OVID'S

Corinna is sensual, worldly, utterly devoted to her delightful avocation. She has appeared in the works of Shakespeare, Marlowe, Robert Herrick, Colette. Her modern counterparts are to be found in Paris or Rome, Madrid or Lisbon.

Ovid writes of sex in a candid spirit. *The Art of Love* is a bold outline of amorous technique; *The Cures for Love* is written in a vein of ironic satire, offering new solutions for those caught up in a hopeless love affair.

Horace Gregory's wise and witty version stresses Ovid's surprisingly modern attitudes toward husbands and wives, infidelity and divorce. The joys of Apollo, Bacchus, and Eros live once more in a language as vibrant and immediate as the original.

"Horace Gregory is a poet and translator of the first order who has also produced a remarkable body of essays and criticism."
—*The Quarterly Review of Literature*

25-A

Other MENTOR Books of Special Interest

THE METAMORPHOSES *by Ovid*
  translated by Horace Gregory
  Ovid's magnificent collection of legends and myths,
  translated into vital modern poetry. (#MQ579—95¢)

THE MENTOR BOOK OF RELIGIOUS VERSE
  edited by Horace Gregory and Marya Zaturenska
  The inspiring poetic treasures of the Western world.
  selected by two experts for their lyric intensity and
  emotional depth, are brought together in this exciting
  volume of religious poetry—taken from ancient times
  to the present day. (#MD189—50¢)

THE SATIRES OF JUVENAL *translated with Introduction*
  by Hubert Creekmore
  All sixteen of Juvenal's mordant satires on the foibles
  of first-century Rome, newly translated by a poet and
  novelist. (#MT535—75¢)

THE SATYRICON *by Petronius*
  translated by William Arrowsmith
  A classic recreation of Nero's pleasure-loving Rome,
  by the cultured cynic, Petronius. In a brilliant new
  translation. (#MP493—60¢)

Love Poems of
OVID

WITHDRAWN

Amores
The Art of Love
The Cures for Love

Selected and in a New English Version
by *Horace Gregory*

A MENTOR CLASSIC

Published by THE NEW AMERICAN LIBRARY

P A
6522
. A 3
1964

FIRST PRINTING, JULY, 1964

Library of Congress Catalog Card Number: 64-21719

MENTOR TRADEMARK REG. U.S. PAT. OFF. AND FOREIGN COUNTRIES
REGISTERED TRADEMARK—MARCA REGISTRADA
HECHO EN CHICAGO. U.S.A.

MENTOR BOOKS are published by
The New American Library of World Literature, Inc.
501 Madison Avenue, New York, New York 10022

PRINTED IN THE UNITED STATES OF AMERICA

For

M. L. Rosenthal

CONTENTS

Preface IX

A Synopsis of the Love Poems of Ovid   XIX

from Amores

BOOK I

Elegy II	The Conqueror Love.............	27
III	The Forthright Lover.............	29
IV	The Dinner Party.................	30
V	A Shady Afternoon...............	34
VII	The Guilty Lover................	35
VIII	The Witch......................	38
IX	Of Soldiers and Lovers...........	43
X	A Tentative Farewell.............	46
XIII	To Aurora......................	49
XIV	The Burning of Her Hair..........	52

BOOK II

Elegy II	To a Eunuch (1).................	57
III	To a Eunuch (2).................	60
IV	The Universal Lover.............	61
VI	Corinna's Parrot.................	64
VII	The Innocent Criminal...........	68
VIII	To Cypassis.....................	70

viii　　　　　　　　*Contents*

XI　Corinna's Voyage.................. 71

XII　Triumph of Love............... 75

XV　The Ring...................... 76

XIX　The Tempted Lover.............. 77

BOOK III

Elegy II　Lady at the Races................ 83

III　Lady Is a Liar.................... 87

V　The Dream..................... 90

X　Homage to Ceres.................. 92

from The Art of Love............................ 97

from The Cures for Love........................117

PREFACE

The love poems in the book that follows this preface were originally inspired and written at the center of a fortunate age in Latin poetry. Horace and Virgil were alive and in high favor, and so were the gifted, slightly lesser-known Propertius and Tibullus. The age was, of course, the Age of Augustus, which is usually dated from the death of Julius Caesar (44 B.C.) to the death of Ovid (A.D. 17). Ovid's *Amores* were among the first of his poems that made him famous.

Ovid (Publius Ovidius Naso) was born in the little town of Sulmo, almost a hundred miles due east of Rome, near the shores of the Adriatic, on March 10th, 43 B.C. His family was of the smaller Italian gentry, of the knighthood class. Although his parents were careful spenders (see *Amores*, Book I, Elegy III), his father was prosperous enough to send him on a "Grand Tour" of the southeast reaches of the Roman world. This included a stay at Athens before he was entered as a student at law in the city of Rome. It was at law school that he was coldly observed by the elder Seneca, father of the philosopher and dramatist, who remarked that young Ovid delivered his pleas with passionate rhetoric rather than with the force of logic.

It is believed that while at school Ovid began the writing and recitation of his *Amores*, and that during these years he gained the friendship of Tibullus and Propertius. Like many young men whose origins may be traced to the provinces, he became more polished, more consciously urban, more Roman at heart than the Romans themselves.

He was more at ease reading his poems to admiring girls and women than he was in a courtroom, where his disregard of formal logic and literal facts as well as his praise of irrational behavior would go unrewarded. In his Elegy XIII, Book I, *Amores*, there is a hint that he was bored by law; at the very least, he shows the weary prospect of lawyers dragged out of bed to plead a case too early in the morning. In the rereading of many of his poems, one feels that his training in law might well have been a first step in his learning how to circumvent it. The kind of advice that Ovid gives to lovers is a genial brushing aside of legal complications—with the hope that true lovers (Elegy XII, Book II) have the wit to outtrick the claims of a Roman husband. In Elegy III, Book I, Ovid cheerfully acknowledged himself as godchild and heir of Bacchus, Eros, and Apollo. Therefore his position was above the law rather than below it. It was as if an irreverent Bill of Rights had been given into his hands by the gods and Muses.

The poets he chose as models were Callimachus and Anacreon, Sappho and Tibullus. Callimachus and Anacreon were poets of great technical proficiency; they excelled in the writing of lightly turned love lyrics and epigrams; Callimachus was famous for his elegies and shafts of satire, Anacreon for his songs in praise of girls and wine. Their importance as teachers of the early Ovid is in their music, their ability to write memorable light verse. (Thomas Moore's versions of Anacreon into Anglo-Irish speech are too closely associated with the drawing-room proprieties of the 1830's to be acceptable today; Anacreon's charming verse, like Moore's, was often shallow.) Ovid's friend and living master was Propertius, whose elegies delighted the rising generation in Roman society and opened the way for the popularity of Ovid's *Amores*. Under these influences and auspices, it is not surprising that Ovid's love elegies became required reading for the extremely gay young friends of Augustus' naughty yet favorite daughter Julia, and *her* daughter, who shared her mother's skill in making love and was also named Julia. The royal Julias led a rout of "emancipated" society girls and matrons—and Ovid's verse flattered their opinions and inclinations. His advice to his patronesses could well have found an echo in Oscar Wilde's remark: "The only way to overcome temptation is to yield to it."

In acknowledging his debts to Sappho and Propertius (whose elegies to Cynthia served as an immediate inspiration for the *Amores*) Ovid placed himself in the line of poets who claimed a descent from the youthful, lyric passions of Catullus: Catullus had translated some few of Sappho's poems into Latin, and Propertius' Cynthia was a latter-day version of Catullus' Lesbia. Ovid's appeal was to a younger generation of readers than those, including Augustus, who had discovered and admired Horace and Virgil. Behind the shafts of Horace's satire stood elder images of pre-Imperial Roman virtue, scenes in which men have hearts that are "triple-bound with brass," and domestic felicities are praised. Horace's praise of living on a Sabine farm showed a worldliness and wit of more sophistication than the urban ironies of the *Amores*, particularly in Elegy IV, Book I, and in Elegy II, Book III.

Ovid's wit was of a totally different temper from that of Horace. It revealed the forces of violent emotions and impulses (shown in Elegy VII, Book I), and the play of its irony takes a turn of exaggerated sentiment in Elegy IV, Book II, of mock anger in the closing lines of Elegy XIII, Book I.

In spite of their youthful display of candor in the art of making love and of their obvious debts to personal experience, the elegies of the *Amores* should not be read in the same spirit with which one reads the opening chapters of an autobiography. Unlike Catullus' Lesbia, the Corinna of Ovid's *Amores* was not a historical personage. The scenes, the people, the episodes of the *Amores* belong to the realities of fiction rather than to those of the confession box. Ovid's Corinna is a composite of many-in-one: she is the living complex of ideal passions, beauties, flaws, fires, tears, and bright-eyed smiles. No less ideal is Corinna's young-man-about-town, the poet named "Ovid," the image of the idle Roman who is blessed or doomed (depending on his mood) by his vocation of forever falling in love.

It is one of the accomplishments of Ovid's genius that

his Corinna and her lover never degenerated into mere stalking-horses performing the act of love on a garishly lighted stage. Somewhat more than life-size in their contours and behavior, they are also creatures of timeless vitality. In Ovid's day they were instantly recognized as fashionable Romans. R. R. Bolgar, in *The Classical Heritage*, tells us how they survived through prescholastic ages, and he suggests that Ovid's characters became ideal pagans. Through those dark centuries Ovidian lovers emerged from the ruins of the ancient world, still covered from head to foot with a sun-engendered golden patina of Roman dust. At the English court of the first Elizabeth, they were the lovers of Christopher Marlowe's version of the *Amores*, tricked out and fashionable again in Elizabethan speech and dress. One also overhears them in lovers' dialogues in Shakespeare's plays. In John Donne's youthful elegies, in his lyrics, there are passages that emulate the restless energy, the ironical reflection, the careless worldliness, the realistic candor of Ovid's hero and heroine. As England's mid-seventeenth century drifted into civil war, Ovid's ideal lovers were reawakened in the pages of Robert Herrick's *Hesperides*. Yet even so, one must not be deceived by mere likeness of a woman's name, for Herrick's Corinna is not Ovid's; when she goes a-Maying, one catches echoes of Horace's half-melancholy Epicurean metaphysics, the kind of warning he offered his Greek girl, Leuconoë, rather than the cheerful blandishments of Ovid:

> We shall grow old apace, and die
> Before we know our liberty.
> Our life is short; and our dayes run
> As fast away as do's the Sunne;
> And as a vapour, or a drop of raine
> Once lost, can ne'r be found againe:
> So when you or I are made
> A fable, song, or fleeting shade;
> All love, all liking, all delight
> Lies drown'd with us in endlesse night.
> Then while time serves, and we are but decaying;
> Come, my Corinna, come, let's goe a Maying.

This is marvelous poetry, but it is not of the kind that
we discover in reading the *Amores*. And yet throughout
the *Hesperides* a diffused association with the lovers of the
Amores is very clear. In both groups of poems the world
is well won or lost for love, and if one seeks out Ovid's
Corinna in Herrick's *Hesperides*, one finds her under the
name of Julia. Even Julia fully clothed has something of
the Roman Corinna's power to attract the senses. She is
bait for Herrick's Ovidian imagination:

> Next, when I cast mine eyes and see
> That brave Vibration each way free;
> O how that glittering taketh me!

Unlike the lovers of the *Amores*, Herrick's almost never
meet in town: there is the literal distance from the Roman
Forum to the English countryside between them. What,
then, so clearly shows a diffusion of the Ovidian spirit in
the *Hesperides*? It is sensuality whose turns of lightness
are inspired by wit. Their delight in the senses is also of
of same vitality; their triumphs of love are actually
triumphs of the life force. When Herrick writes, "The
sweets of love are mixt with tears," he has the authority
of Ovid behind him, and the same authority sustains him
as he says,

> Let faire or foule my Mistresse be,
> Or low, or tall, she pleaseth me:
> Or let her walk, or stand, or sit,
> The posture hers, I'm pleased with it.
> Or let her tongue be still, or stir,
> Gracefull is ev'ry thing from her.

In these lines there is no doubt of Ovidian cheerfulness.
If on occasion Herrick permitted Horace to do his think-
ing for him, he reserved the granting of special praise to
Ovid in "The Apparition of his Mistresse calling him to
ELIZIUM:"

> . . . witty Ovid, by
> Whom faire Corinna sits, and doth comply
> With Yvorie wrists, his Laureat head, and steeps
> His eye in dew of kisses, while he sleeps.

Through the poetry of Dryden, Swift, and Pope, Ovid continued to be an important source of inspiration. Until the middle of the eighteenth century he was greatly valued as "a poets' poet." In the schools, however, Horace and Virgil rose above him in favor. In the nineteenth century, and during the long reign of Victorian circumlocutions, the candid and comic spirit of Ovid's lovers dropped below the level of propriety and out of fashion. Even the reading of Christopher Marlowe's richly textured version of the *Amores* was half-forbidden. Their great offense was in making light of sex—therefore Ovid was set aside in darkened corners of bookshelves to await a rediscovery.

Today Ovid has come back into circulation. Readers are more understanding than their great-grandfathers were of Ovidian attitudes—toward husbands, toward social status, toward money and divorce. It is in both the conflicts and harmonies, the resemblances and contrasts of these attitudes with respect to ours, that the timelessness of Ovid's lovers makes itself felt today. To recognize the presence of his girls and women one has only to remember that they are of Latin blood and temperament, that they are more likely to be living in Paris or Rome, Madrid or Lisbon, than in London or New York. We can see their cousinship to the women in Colette's novels, and to the heroines (the stars!) of Italian motion pictures—who are noted both for their sex appeal and practical behavior. It is the lover who pays, and not the mistress. If the lover can't afford her, the loss is his, not hers.

Elegy VIII of Book I has a fantastic, yet memorable character in Madame Dipsas—or, rather, Madame Drink. Though she seems thoroughly ensconced within a Roman brothel of Ovid's day, she is of a sisterhood that Colette revealed with gray-eyed candor and compassionate understanding. Though Colette's voracious readings probably never included the Elegies, one can say that the novels of Colette and the *Amores* stem from an identical tradition. Both of their authors observed and held to the Latin conventions of the demimonde. Colette's girls and women are as richly dressed, or as richly naked, as Ovid's. Their way of life (for which they expect to be well paid) is the

Art of Love. Gigi has an aunt as conscious of the right clothes, the right jewels to wear, as Ovid was in advising women how to dress.

Colette's *The Last of Cheri* has distinctly Ovidian overtones. Cheri himself is the reflected image of Narcissus-Hermaphroditus from the *Metamorphoses;* his middle-aged mistress, Lea, is very like the eager, always yielding, all-embracing nymph Salmacis. They exist among the diffused, yet living particles of a Latin heritage in fiction and poetry. In *The Last of Cheri* Madame Drink is not Cheri's mistress, but is one of her friends, whose *nom de guerre* is Pal. With her fondness for drink she acquired the habit of smoking opium. To her gifts of prophesy she added a pack of tarot cards. Like Madame Drink she is a witch, and, again like her, she wears a comic mask through which she utters dogmas of practical criticism and wisdom.

In his complaint against Madame Drink, Ovid's young lover loses his temper, yet the shades of difference between Ovid's portrait of her and Colette's are not those of tolerance, but rather of degrees in worldliness. Contrasted with Colette's transcendent, Minerva-like poise in presenting her characters, Ovid's young lover and his abusive anger seem naïve. In bringing Ovid and Colette together in what may seem a curious alliance (but one less strange if we remember that many of her themes are related to scenes of women falling in and out of love), the very least that we can say is that Ovid knew, far earlier than she, the crooked turns of emotion, the conflicting logics, the hopes, desires that are at the source of human comedy.

On the surface it would seem that Ovid's lovers had booked (as early as a dozen years before the birth of Christ) charter membership in a twentieth-century cult of violence. Nothing could be further from the truth. In the *Amores* Ovid's scenes of violence are fuel for comedy, not romantic melodrama. His lovers are carried through violent stages of joy, guilt, sexual rapture, and jealousy: the yielding mistress becomes a harping fury (Elegy VII, Book II), and the loyal lover suddenly turns into a creature who is attracted by every girl he sees (Elegy IV,

Book II). With rapid changes of moods and tempers, the lovers become enchanted monsters of infidelity.

In Elegy VII, Book I, the girl who survives a beating from her lover is calm enough; she is not too badly hurt; she would never do as a Queen of Tragedy. The episode carries with it psychological force and penetration. Ovid's wit is directed against Mars, and with a further turn of ironic brilliance, he reveals the violence of Cupid—which is a vastly different kind of violence from that of twentieth-century impulses toward self-destruction—and he makes this distinction clear in his address to Cupid at the beginning of *The Cures for Love*.

In his essay "The Metamorphoses of Violence in Titus Andronicus," Professor Eugene M. Waith remarks that Ovid's concern was "in the transforming power of intense states of emotion." Although the behavior of Ovid's lovers seems to foreshadow the magnificent transformation scenes in his *Metamorphoses*, scenes of violence in the *Amores* are in the spirit of Shakespeare's *A Midsummer Night's Dream* and are purged by wit.

Between the writing of his love poems and the work of his later years, a semitragic metamorphosis from urban poet to poet-in-exile had taken place. By order of the Emperor Augustus, Ovid and his poems were banished from the city of Rome.

The emperor's banishment of Ovid in A.D. 8 to Tomis on the shores of the Black Sea is surrounded by rumors, legends, speculations. Ovid in his autobiographical *Tristia* and *Epistulae ex Ponto*, written in self-defense after Augustus' sentence was imposed, displays bewilderment, self-pity, and a sense of guilt, yet he obscures the reasons why the emperor turned against him. In the *Tristia* Ovid falls out of character; he has no authority as a weeping hero. Hermann Frankel, in his *Ovid: A Poet Between Two Worlds*, believes that Augustus banished Ovid and his books on charges of *Majestas* or *lèse-majesté*, that his books, particularly *The Art of Love*, published in 2 B.C., offended the dignity of the Roman state and, in the emperor's eyes, contributed to the deliquency of girls and matrons. A.D. 8 was also the year that Augustus brought charges of adultery against his granddaughter Julia and exiled her—and because of this coincidence in time and because it was known that she was among the poet's admirers, it has been supposed that Ovid was then forced to share ("guilt by association") the blame for her misconduct. But, as Dr. Frankel warns us, these efforts to explain Augustus' action are speculations, not established motives for his behavior.

In line with the speculations of Dr. Frankel, Suetonius reported a speech Augustus made to the people of Rome defending the exile of his daughter Julia: "May the gods curse you with daughters as lecherous as mine, and with wives as adulterous!" The statement is proof enough of the emperor's grief and anger as well as his disgust at the moral conduct of his household. Offended dignity is also evident—and it is probable that Ovid's irreverent attitude toward the conventions of domestic morality aroused the emperor's displeasure. Though he, like Ovid, had been divorced twice and was living, as he neared seventy, with his third wife, he was coldly critical of the younger generation; and it is possible that he sought for and found in Ovid the nearly perfect scapegoat.

Exiled to Tomis, a town on the Euxine in the land (modern Romania) of the Getae, Ovid retouched, some people say, the final draft of his masterpiece, the *Metamorphoses*. It was there that he continued writing the *Fasti* and his complaint, his long *Tristia*. His writings were never again to equal the refreshing lyricism of the *Amores* and the storytelling verve of the *Metamorphoses*. He died at sixty, yet, for many years after his death rumors flowed southward down from Tomis, speaking of how he had charmed the savage Getae by writing poems in their language. It was said he had become their poet laureate.

As for the present version of Ovid's love poems, it is a selection of elegies from his *Amores* as well as a choice of candid passages from his *Art of Love* and *Cures for Love*, made with the hope of showing the youthful Ovid at his best, of displaying his wit, his sensuality, his irony, his lyrical beauty, his passionate intensities. Such is the hope that exists behind the making of this book: but as all of us know, poetry belongs to the language in which it is written, and no twentieth-century version of the elegies in English can equal their originals in Latin. My version is an attempt to re-create their immediacy, their lightness, their spontaneity, their polish. The selection seeks to relieve the text of its repetitions of mood and action as well as its areas of dullness. Elegy VII, Book III, is omitted because Dean Swift in his "Celia" poems and in his "Progress of Beauty" can best please readers who enjoy the satiated Ovid; in place of it I have chosen lines from *The Cures for Love* to represent Ovid's lover discovering his mistress at her toilette.

The liberties I have taken with the Latin text have led to fewer sins of omission than those of expansion. Certain allusions, familiar enough to Ovid's contemporaries, would perhaps seem both elliptical and obscure to modern readers; I have thought it better to explain them by adding a phrase or two within the body of the English version than to clutter the bottom of the page with footnotes.

I have also taken the liberty of giving the elegies titles so that the reader may identify them by referring to the table of contents.

For encouragement in my writing a new version of Ovid's love poems my thanks are due to Norman Holmes Pearson and Patrick Gregory. For a first reading of the book in manuscript and for his salutary strictures I am deeply grateful to Dudley Fitts. I also have a special debt of gratitude to Arabel Porter and Victor Weybright of New American Library for their patience and understanding.

H. G.

Palisades, New York
July 15th, 1963

AMORES

BOOK I:

Elegy I opens the book with the statement that its author intended to write of war, but Love prevented his writing heroic verse by stealing a metrical foot from every other line. (This is probably written with an ironic smile in the direction of Virgil's opening line of his *Aeneid:* "Of arms and the man, I sing".) Therefore, Ovid becomes Love's poet.

Elegies II, III, IV, and V are in my version of the text.

Elegy VI is a long address to the bolt which locks a lady's door against her lover. The second and third elegies of Book II are more dramatic versions of the lover's frustrations, and these are included in my text.

Elegies VII and VIII are in my text.

So are Elegies IX and X.

Elegies XI and XII are on the theme of writing letters to Corinna.

Elegies XIII and XIV are in my text and XIV illustrates Ovid's great charm in the writing of his particular kind of light verse.

Elegy XV is on the subjects of envy and immortality, which are treated with greater art, feeling, and distinction in Ovid's *Metamorphoses*.

BOOK II:

Elegy I speaks of the poet's effort to open his lady's door by means of his gift for writing poetry.

Elegies II, III, and IV are in my text.

Elegy V is the lover's complaint that someone else has taught his mistress new tricks in making love. His jealousy (Elegy IV, Book I) is shown more vividly in the earlier poem.

Elegy VI, included in my text, was brilliantly reworked into a satire ("Speak, Parrot") on the court of Henry VIII, by John Skelton. With less assurance than the knowledge of Skelton's debt to Ovid, one may also fancy that Ovid's elegy on a parrot is the distant ancestor of the nursery rhyme on the death and burial of Cock Robin.

Elegies VII and VIII are in my text.

Elegies IX and X are two complaints: IX, against Love; X, the complaint of the lover trapped between the attractions of two ladies.

Elegies XI and XII are in my text.

Elegy XIII is on Corinna's pregnancy, a theme that Ovid treats with less than his usual skill, nor is his commentary on women who kill their infants (Elegy XIV) more fortunate.

Elegy XV is in my text, and it is highly probable that Shakespeare remembered it when he wrote the balcony scene in *Romeo and Juliet*. It would also seem that in his "A Jett Ring sent," John Donne transformed Ovid's images into metaphysical brilliants.

Elegy XVI is a complaint: the lover is at home in Sulmo and unhappily away from Corinna and Rome.

Elegy XVII is on his difficult relations with Corinna, and Elegy XVIII is a variation of his theme of being a follower of Love rather than of Mars.

Elegy XIX is in my text.

BOOK III:

Elegy I is a mock debate (and too long-winded) between the Elegiac Muse and the Muse of Tragedy—and Elegy wins.

Elegies II and III are in my text.

In Elegy IV, Ovid repeats his earlier warnings to stupid husbands.

Elegy V is in my text.

Elegy VI is a river elegy—but Ovid in his *Metamorphoses* is a far better poet of rivers and at his best in the story of Io.

Elegy VII is in my text.

Elegy VIII is a complaint against a money-loving mistress.

Elegy IX is a tribute to the poet Tibullus. In my text of *The Cures for Love*, Ovid pays tribute to a number of poets, Tibullus among them.

Elegy X is in my text.

Elegy XI is still another complaint, and the remaining four elegies are farewells to love.

THE ART OF LOVE

and

THE CURES FOR LOVE

Ovid's notes on cosmetics (*De Medicamina Faciei*), his *Art of Love*, and his *Cures for Love* show his wit in writing mock-didactic verse. Because his didactic poems are repetitious, it is well to represent them by the boldest of their instructions. Therefore, the present text omits the notes on cosmetics in favor of Ovid's rules on how women should dress, and these lines are chosen from *The Art of Love*. If they are extended at too great length, even the best of didactic poems tend to lull their readers to sleep —and why? Because the desire to preach and to give gratuitous advice too often transforms the poet into the teacher—and when that happens, Apollo and Dionysus fly out of the window.

When Ovid concluded his *Cures for Love*, he was almost ready to begin writing the *Metamorphoses*, in which the adventures of young women in love transcended whatever advice he had to offer.

FROM AMORES

BOOK

I

THE CONQUEROR LOVE

What does this mean? With everything gone
    wrong?
My bed hopeless and hard,
coverlet and blanket fallen to the floor—
no sleep at all throughout the endless night
while every bone in my poor twisted body
cries out in pain?
Am I attacked by Love before I know it?
The subtle sickness?
That's it: invisible arrows in my heart;
merciless Love is here to tear my breast.

Shall I give in to him?
Or fight his flames that wake to fire in me?
Suppose I lie down flat—
to those who wear pain lightly, pain is nothing!
When torches move, their fires leap to heaven—
if someone drops a torch, the flames die out.
The ox who balks, who tries to wreck his harness,
gets nastier blows than one who likes to plow;
the rearing stallion has blood at his lips
while others take the bit and scarcely feel it.
Unwilling lovers wear ferocious burns;
their wounds run deeper
than those who are Love's Prisoners of War.

Take me at once—since I'm your victim, Cupid,
my hands wait for your chains.
I cannot fight. I pray for peace, for pardon,
but you must dress at once for war, for battle.
Don't take me as you are,
both of us standing naked and disarmed!
Put on your wreath of myrtle as a crown,
harness your mother's doves.
Stepfather Mars'll let you take his car
where millions praise
the charioteer who steers a brace of birds!
And for your greater triumph,
your followers are handsome boys and girls—
and here am I, the latest,
showing my recent wounds and wearing chains,
happy to be enslaved.
Stripped Prudery shall have hands tied behind her,
so shall False Shame who blushes without reason,
so shall all enemies,
all who resist Love's army in the field.
And all shall fear Lord Cupid
and cry out in a great voice: "VICTORY,
IO, VICTORY!" while at your side
are Blandishments, all the soft words of Love,
behind them, Madness, Error,
Love's noncommissioned officers on duty
who pillage Gods and men,
and yet without them Cupid always fails.
Joy in your triumph!
Your mother showers praises from Olympus,
and from her altars
rose petals fall upon your blessed head,
and on your wings and hair,
diamonds and pearls, yourself a golden boy
riding in light above your glittering car.
And if I know you well,
your fires blaze among the cheering crowds,
wounds everywhere—
as you pass by, the air is filled with arrows.
Yours was the way Bacchus had conquered Asia:
his terrible tigers came—

your doves inspire the same wild wake of terror.
Since I'm completely yours,
a pious prisoner of Love forever,
don't spend your strength on me—
O Cupid, spare me now, now and tomorrow:
think of the conquests of your Cousin Caesar,
whose hand protects the victims of his power!

ELEGY III

THE FORTHRIGHT LOVER

I swear I do not ask too much of heaven:
O make that thoughtless girl
who yesterday made me her spoils of war
either love me
or let me share her bed to prove I love her.
I ask too much too soon? Then I beg pardon!
(I hope she doesn't run away to hide.)
O Cytherea, hear my countless prayers!

And now my dear, my darling,
accept no lesser love than mine forever.
I'm at your feet, your servant:
take me who knows what love and loyalty mean.
My name's not ancient,
for the first Naso was of lesser gentry—
he rode his horse and ran a small plantation.
My parents saved their money:
yet God Apollo and his nine sweet Muses,
and after them, great Bacchus,
even Love, Himself, have made me what I am,
and Love so fashioned me
that I'm his priceless gift to girls like you!

Unlike most men, I always keep my word:
my manners—excellent,

stylish, yet unaffected and sincere.
I am (although I almost blush to say it)
a forthright man!
A thousand women hold no interest for me.
One in a thousand
shall be the girl I love. Love makes me faithful.

I know the Fates have spun our destinies,
mine into yours forever:
and you shall weep for me when I am dead—
and I? I'll make you live in poetry,
my deathless heroine;
all that I write will be the better for it.
The poem makes the girl:
once Io feared to find herself a cow;
Leda was frightened
when she, against her will, took on the swan,
so was Europa riding out to sea—
she held the bull's horns in her girlish hands!
So shall our lives grow famous in a poem
known round the world—your name as bright as
    mine.

ELEGY IV

THE DINNER PARTY

Tonight, drinks at a party: we'll be there—
your husband, too!
I hope tonight's his last—he's better dead!
(And what of me? Am I a harmless guest,
staring at her I love? The one who sees
her lean a naked shoulder to his breast
to keep him warm?)
And must I see his hands
glide down your neck, down to that secret place
where he can take his pleasure at his will?

When wine poured free,
no wonder Hippodamia
was forced to fight the Centaurs who came at
    her—
she was like you!
Though I'm no monster of the shady forest,
half horse, half man,
how can I keep my hands from stripping you
naked as dawn to hold you in my arms?

And now, my dear, instructions for tonight,
follow my words, nor let them fall away,
tossed to the mad East Wind or lukewarm South!
Before your husband comes,
walk in to join us—
what next? I'm not quite clear—but get there
    first—
then, as he takes his place,
steer down beside him, innocent and cool,
your naked foot on mine beneath the table.
Gaze in my eyes,
read what they have to say!
Each move I make is yours to read, to follow.
Look, I incline my head,
I raise an eyebrow: these are words, my dear,
words without sounds—and when the drinks are
    served
across the table
I'll write "I love you" in spilled drops of wine.
Then answer me in kind: if you remember
how joyfully, how well we mount each other,
drunk with delights of Venus
in my bed,
then touch your glowing cheeks with one slow
    finger.
Or if you have unspoken doubts about me,
stroke your right earlobe with indifferent hand.

Light of my life! If what I say disarms you,
start twirling that jet ring that holds your finger,
and then as though

your hands were placed in prayer
lean on the table
which means you hope your husband's damned
    to hell—
perfect reward for everything he does!
And when he mixes wine for you, be clever,
tell him it's delicious—
perfect for him, but far too rich for you—
and have him drink it!
Ask the wine steward for your choice,
then drink,
and where your lips have touched the brim, I'll
    kiss.
We'll drink together!
Don't let him feed you from his plate. Don't let
his arms encircle you, nor your fair head
lean toward his heavy shoulder,
nor his hands
play at the rose-tipped nipples of your breasts.
And now in public,
don't let his lips touch yours—if you forget
I'll tell him to his face
that I'm your lover,
I'll say, "Those kisses belong to me!" and prove it.

It's more than probable all this will happen,
yet what I cannot hope
to see is worse—
it is what he does to you beneath your cloak:
don't let your naked thigh touch his, nor move
your slender feet
against his foot—all this
is what I fear. I know how well we've played
that game of hide and seek
when no one saw us—
a quick and easy way to come together—
your cloak was like a little tent around us!
Now let it drop:
it hides too many secrets.
And make your husband drink: give him straight
    drinks,

but never kisses, let him sink in wine,
blind, sleeping drunk—
now we can talk of plans:
as others rise to go, slip through the crowd,
and make your way toward home—
I'll move with others.
Perhaps you'll miss me,
or I'll look for you, half-lost—
then suddenly, your hand upon my arm!

Even our joys in bed are far too brief—
at midnight
you become his prisoner;
your husband locks the door; the Night divides us,
and I, Night's Outcast,
weep my futile tears.
Of course, the brute will take you in his arms,
and kiss you, more than kiss you—
mount you straightly
until he has his husbandly reward,
the very joy we shared two hours before!
Then as he enters you,
nor speak, nor murmur,
nor make your small and sweetly yielding cries:
let him discover that your mound of Venus
can show distemper,
that even its warmly flowing eager fountain
has now run dry.

(If there is anyone to hear my prayers,
I pray he has no pleasure
when he takes her,
and that her fond delight in pleasing men
turns to indifference
when she feels him near.)

However Fortune turns her wheel tonight
tell me tomorrow (with a steady voice)
even the sheets grew cold as you surrendered.

ELEGY V

A SHADY AFTERNOON

A humid day: a shady afternoon:
my limbs fell where the couch sank to embrace
    me.
The blinds drawn fast—except
one that swayed open, and in poured false light,
light of green forests,
half-light that falters, fades as Phoebus leaves us,
or as Night turns to Dawn:
the kind of light that should hide timid girls—
if they're undressed and hope that no one's near.
Yet look! Here comes Corinna
in her chemise that flutters as she moves:
her hair floats to her shoulders—
in that brave style Semiramis was dressed
to cross the threshold to her wedding bed.
And so was Lais dressed—
that pretty quean who pleased so many men.

I ripped her shift, so very thin it was
it scarcely flawed the beauty under it,
and she fought hard to gather it around her,
to win a foolish battle—
then she gave in—which was her self-betrayal!
Her frail chemise had vanished:
she stood before me more than beautiful.
How could I fail to praise her arms, her shoulders!
And O her waiting breasts
erect for kisses. . . . And that fair field below
    them!

34

What long and lovely flanks, what girlish thighs!
But why say more? All that I saw
was in my arms, was perfect. I took her naked.
And what did we do next? Who does not know?
Worn out, we had a brief, but deep siesta.
O give me many afternoons like this!

ELEGY VII

THE GUILTY LOVER

Lock up my hands—my hands are murderous!
O doctors, friends!
Have I friends here?
Then roll me up in chains until the madness
that curses both my hands is drained away!
O my poor girl—
my treacherous hands tore at her,
stripped her half-naked
and almost knocked her down—
her bruises show beneath a rain of tears:
such hands are hands that would have whipped
      my parents,
or lashed out at the Gods.

                    Am I insane?
Didn't wild Ajax of the seven-plated shield
strike down a herd of cattle in a pasture?
Didn't Orestes
follow up crime with crime
murd'ring his mother after she killed his father—
that done, he tried to war against the Furies?
And because they had their way,
have I the right
to let my hands fly at her face and shoulder?

                        Yet, with her hair

undone, she looks so lovely!
                        Less trim, less perfect,
but more beautiful!
She looks like Atalanta at the hunt—
she's also like the weeping girl of Crete
who saw the South Wind drive away to sea
the ships, the sails, the hopes, the promises
that lying Theseus made her heart remember.
And though that lady
dressed her hair with ribbons,
she's very like Cassandra when she fell
at your white feet, O Puritan Minerva!

Who was the girl who found no words to say,
"Have you gone mad?
Look at the beast—he's crazy!"
The girl said nothing: terror clipped out her
        tongue—
yet her face spoke against me—
and quick tears
told me my guilt.
                    My friends, look at my arms—
then cut them off. Rather than see her tears
I'd maim myself and prove my foolish strength
by tearing at the limbs of my foul body.
What are my hands?
These hands are not myself,
but gangsters hired out for midnight murders.
Put them in irons—
and if my fists knocked down a Roman beggar,
both judge and jury
would send me off to cool my hands in jail.
Do I walk free
because I struck a girl?
Diomedes swung wide to strike at Venus—
the conduct of delinquent Gods and men!
And I repeat his error—
another hero
with less excuse than he, I slapped her face
because I love the girl—
while Diomedes fought an enemy.

Since I'm a hero, these are my commands
to guide myself,
to march in proper glory: "Wear your laurels!
Light up the fires to Jove!
You'll hear the cries
of multitudes beside your chariot wheels:
'Follow our King, our Prince of Conquerors,
who won the war against his silent girl!'
Then have her walk before you,
hair undone,
her body white except where purple bruises
have stained her skin—your slave, your prisoner!"

(On that fair skin it would have been far better
to draw blood with my kisses,
to bite—but no!
My blood runs wild and swells in roaring rivers;
when anger takes me, I'm all storm and fury.)
It would have been enough to scold the girl,
then stroke her trembling thighs—
instead of shouting that I'd take her life,
I should have torn away
the other half
of her chemise—her clinging girdle would have
shown her more naked than disarmed and
          frightened.
But I did not. My hands were at her face,
that gentle face
that showed her birth, her breeding,
her look of freedom!

She stood there, dazed,
white as Parian marble,
trembling as poplars shimmer when light winds
          take them,
or as a reed vibrates
when Zephyr passes,
or as a wave stirs when the South Wind warms it.

Yet she held back the tears that brimmed her eyes,
then as a melting snowbank

turns to water,
her tears began to flood that lovely face,
and I began to feel
guilt turn within me
as though my very blood flowed in her weeping.

Three times I tried to ask her to forgive me:
I kissed her feet—
she thrust away my hands.
And now, my dear, show pity, ease my pain—
tear at my face, my lips, my eyes, my hair:
if hands are weak,
passion will give them fire!
And then to hide your bruises and my sorrow,
lift up your arms to braid your winding hair.

ELEGY VIII

THE WITCH

—And do you know a bitch who owns a road-
    house?
Listen to me: her name is Mistress Drink—
that's what she should be called—
she's always drunk.
Even when rose-colored horses of the morning
fly through the sky
she's still blind drunk, or else she's drunk again—
and yet she knows black arts and Circe's magic:
she charms wild waters at their secret springs.
O but she's clever!
She knows strange herbs and roots that cure or kill
and how the Great Wheel spins
our thread of life in years, or breaks it short.
She knows what makes the mare attract her lover!

And as she wills it,
storm clouds black out the heavens and day is
  night,
or, at her fancy, night is day again.
When she is near, I've seen the stars rain blood,
blood streaming down the face of ancient Luna!
I half suspect
she flies across the night while all her body
is feathered like an owl's.
I'm almost certain, for a rumor tells me,
her eyes have double lenses shooting fire—
that she calls out the dead
from immemorial tombs, then canyon-deep
(with scarlet runes and devil-haunted curses)
she splits the earth!

And that great creature trapped the girl I love.
(We'd just begun a pleasant
love affair
with promises to spend the night together.)
One must admit the creature's filthy style
was eloquent! (I stepped behind her door
and overheard it.)
"Light of my eyes," she said, "you're ravishing!
That rich boy always comes to look at you:
he stands and stares!
You're wonderful—that's why—
of course, you know it!
But O my dear, don't wear that shabby dress!
Your looks demand the best. Expensive beauties
are always girls who wear expensive clothes.
You're generous, too,
for when he makes you rich, I won't be poor.
Let's see: your most unlucky star is Mars—
now Mars is out of sight,
Venus is rising, and she'll bring you millions!
Today, the rich boy comes—of course he loves
  you:
he knows what beauty needs!
He's handsome, and you'd make a lovely couple!
Even if he wasn't rich, you'd almost pay him

to have him mount you for an hour in bed."
(My girl began to blush.) "That's the right color
and for white skin like yours, it's very pretty—
the blush that comes and goes
should be true art: it always brings in money.
But shamefaced blushes are a stupid loss.
Now, Lovey, bend your head:
eyes on your lap—that's right! It's there you see
how much a lover gives you. . . . In Tatius' day
the unwashed Sabine girls
had one man each—one husband—that was all!
Today (through foreign wars) men get more
          restless,
and Venus rules the city of her Aeneas.
Our Roman beauties
are ripe and often love to play all night.
The shy girl's not sought out, yet if she's smart
(provincial tricks have fallen
out of vogue),
she makes advances—and she never frowns!
Don't spoil your forehead—make your wrinkles
          vanish—
and now, my dear, a smile—
you need a cheerful lack of inhibitions!

"Penelope took measure of young men:
she tested all their powers with the bow
(which she held in her hand)
and good stiff horn was sure to pierce her target!

"The best of life streams by before we know it:
Time gathers speed,
and round the circus, months and years have
          flown!
Yet bronze the more you use it takes on bright-
          ness:
fine clothes need wearing,
but a deserted house falls gray with ruin.
Beauty's warm portals should be opened wide:
if not, her doors fall shut with age and rust.
One man or two? That's not enough!

The more you have, the less you owe the giver.
The wise wolf counts her sheep: one herd, one
    dinner.

"Think hard, my dear:
you say your poet pays you with his verses?
No more, and that is all? Poor, foolish girl!
You're worth a thousand lines a day from lovers!

"Wearing his golden cloak,
Apollo, God of poets, rules the city:
he plucks the strings and sounds a golden echo
which Roman beauties hear.
The kind of poet worthy of attention
should write twice Homer's lines in golden
    talents—
to give so much Is genius!
And don't despise the newly rich: make sure
they pay you well . . .
nor let Young Gentry show his family portraits:
his ancestors are dead; forget their statues:
they won't support you if Young Gentry's poor!
Don't take a pretty boy
who thinks he's paid you if you share his pleasure.
Ask him how much he earns from his rich lovers!

"Yet as you stretch your net
don't ask too much at first—some birds take
    flight—
but lead them to the bush, then quote your price.

"A simulated love
won't chill his ardor: make him love you dearly.
The while his money flows you're his forever.
Often say, 'Not tonight':
you have a headache, but the best excuse is
'The Wrong Time of the Month,' for Isis rules
    you!
Then take him by surprise:
be swift, be urgent,
or he'll get used to missing you in bed.

If you say 'No' too long his penis dwindles.

"Deafen your doors to fools who talk too much:
open them wide to soldierly attack!
Let him hear how virile
your absent lover is—if he gets angry,
unleash your temper first: claw at his eyes—
even his earliest counterblows will fail.
A good hot quarrel
should never last too long: Love's death is in it.
Learn how to make
your eyes flow raining tears down cheeks and
        breasts,
and teach yourself to lie: Venus won't hear you.
Make all your friends
tell lovers what to buy you: in that list
to name gifts for themselves, then give them to
        you.
Enough straws, such as these,
will build a mountain: gifts for Aunt Helen,
for Darling Nurse, for Treasured Mother—the
        total rises:
your gifts should seem to fall
from everywhere: and when the round of giving
slows down at last, say sweetly, 'It's my birthday:
the cake is here. We'll both sit down to eat.'

"Don't let a lover rest:
hint of new lovers and their charms in bed:
love dies of boredom when it feels secure.
Show him how others kiss,
the secret places where they love to bite,
the bruises round your neck—then show the
        presents
that others send you. If he is slow to follow
whatever you may mean, take him outdoors
to stroll with him through fashionable shops—
The Sacred Way is where you'll find the best.
If he complains
and says he's short of cash, make him use credit,
then open charge accounts made in his name.

If you mistrust your man,
fondle him sweetly:
remember honey blandishes our ills!
O I have long, long thoughts,
not for the wind, but for the girl who listens:
such girls'll worship me beyond my death
and raise an altar where my bones find rest."
That was her talk—
till suddenly my shadow crossed the lattice—
I had leaned out too far.
My hands were hot to tear the withered straw
she wore as hair, to slap her wine-soaked eyes,
and wreck that map of wrinkles called her face . . .
yet I ran home.

O Mistress Bottle—Mistress Brandy—Mistress
  Drink!
May the Great Gods rot your teeth and send you
  homeless
to wander everlasting fields of snow—
and never a drop of liquor in that desert.

ELEGY IX

OF SOLDIERS AND LOVERS

All lovers stand erect as men of war:
Cupid has headquarters,
his troops around him—
believe me, Greeks, each lover is a soldier.
When war comes into fashion,
so does Venus!
Old men are feeble soldiers, fuddling lovers:
what the top sergeant looks for in a fighter,
girls look for in a man—
action at night.

The sentry keeps
his captain's tent in view—
the lover's sleepless eye, his sweetheart's door.
The trooper never fails
his marching orders—
however far a woman takes a journey,
her lover follows her to ends of earth:
he climbs glass mountains,
he wades great rivers
that spread around him in a flood of rain.
And where the mountaintops
are glazed with snow,
he strides through storms, or if he's out at sea,
he battles rough winds through
an eastern tempest.
Nor does he speak of hardship anywhere,
but steers his course by gazing at the stars.
Who other than a lover
or a soldier
braves dark, frostbitten nights through hail and
    snow?
One matches wits
with wary enemies:
the other keeps an eye on clever rivals.
One mans the siege
against a rock-walled city:
the other entrance to a strong-willed girl.
One climbs through bedroom windows to show
    valor,
the other forces city gates ajar.
The best attack is:
take them while they're sleeping—
your sword in hand against a naked foe.
That's how Odysseus and Diomedes
came against Rhesus on the Trojan plain,
stole his white horses,
and left him dead upon the conquered field.
So lovers take advantage of the night:
while husbands sleep, their swords are driven
    home.
Whether he's a soldier,

or an unwanted lover,
the breakthrough is his duty and reward.

Sometimes Mars sways the battle left and right,
and victory's in doubt,
and it's well known that Venus often wavers:
sometimes the loser
rises from defeat
to conquer those who say they'll never fall.
Though some fools say
love has no "fighting spirit,"
love always proves its genius at white heat:
when Briseis was stolen from his side
the great Achilles
was a pillar of flame—
the Trojans had to fight as best they could!
From his wife's arms Hector went hot to war—
she fixed his headgear as he strode away.
And Agamemnon,
greatest of commanders,
stood dazzled at the sight of bright Cassandra
who like a Maenad shook her floating hair.
And Mars in mounting Venus was caught naked
in Vulcan's net
where both went on display—
while their performance was the talk of heaven!

Till recently I spent my time at ease
in country quiet,
in this green shade I dreamed and wrote my
        verses . . .
then fire caught me . . . for the loveliest girl
waked me to strategy.
I am no coward!
Action at night shall always be my glory.
If you would keep your sword up—
and your spirit—then fall in love!

A TENTATIVE FAREWELL

As she (I speak of Helen snatched by Paris)
sailed the Eurotas
in a Phrygian ship,
and then was cause of war between her men—
like Leda she was tricked
by a swift lover—
Leda's was white and seemed to be a bird—
before she'd caught her breath he was upon her
and held her fast—
as Amymone walked drought-withered sands,
erect, an urn of water on her head,
she could neither turn nor run
while Neptune mounted her and had his will—
as innocent as these
I thought *you* were,
but not today. And O I loved you dearly:
I feared the Eagle
and the wandering Bull,
disguises that Jove wears in raping girls—
a girl like you.
But now my fears are gone—farewell my fancies!
Your beauty's not reflected in my eyes:
Do you want the reason why?
You're too expensive: a price for *this*, a price for
      doing *that*—
and if we go to bed!
Good Jove, a fortune!
When you were sweet and shy and natural
O how I loved you—
spirit and flesh in one, and all in all.
Your calculating heart has spoiled your looks.

Love is an innocent,
a naked boy.
Why ask the heir of Venus to think of money?
Since he's undressed, he carries no loose change:
Venus & Son are not among those troops
who march in line for pay,
for if they did, where is their Godliness?

The call girl in a whorehouse
has her duties;
she takes on any man who pays her wages
and curses those who split the profits with her—
she has appointments,
you have love affairs,
the right to choose the man you love the best.
Although they seem to lack an urban charm,
learn natural courtesy
from Nature's children
who are less worldly than you seem to be.
Look at the creatures grazing in the pasture:
young mares and stallions,
frisky cows and bulls;
the females never think of taking money,
nor does the pink-eared ewe
expect a fortune when she meets the ram.
Only a woman takes pride in the fleecing
of men who spend the night with her in bed,
and only women sell
the wealth, the pleasure
they wear between their legs, the joy, the rapture
of girls and men.
The kind of love which Venus offers man,
man takes from woman till both in love's delight
are held at last in one another's arms—
why should girls sell such treasure
or men buy it?
Why should my ecstasies drive me toward ruin,
while all your pleasures
make you sleek and rich?
Here is delight that men and women give
each to the other when they meet in bed.

Money buys witnesses and crooked lawyers;
money corrupts the judge,
the case, the jury—
but worse than these are girls who think their love,
their joy of life,
their very beauty are trinkets bought and sold.
Things that are given freely win devotion—
no thanks are owed
to girls who sell themselves at fancy prices,
and he who pays the fee has closed his bargain.
Therefore, my beauties,
learn that love is priceless,
that taint of money turns all love to dust:
No good came to Tarpeia,
Vestal virgin,
who sold her honor for bright Sabine bracelets—
she thought that armbands welded to a shield
were good as gold—then as she slipped them on,
her bones were crushed
beneath their brass-bound weight.
Knowing her husband would be killed at Thebes
(bribed by a necklace),
damned Eriphyle
sent him to death, and when her son learned of it,
his sword ran through the belly that gave him
        birth—
she knew too late the price her necklace brought.

But if you long for diamonds and rubies,
go get them from the very, very rich—
wherever money grows
take all you can—
there, where the grapes hang heavy, make your
        choice—
gather your golden apples
from an orchard
as rich as Alcinous showed Odysseus.
Then, when your lover's
not a millionaire,
take your gratuities in Faithfulness,
in Ardor,

in all his pretty Arts that please a mistress.

My gifts to girls are certain lovely poems,
and if I choose,
my songs make women famous—
the lucky girls immortalized by me!

Your evening gowns soon wear away to rags;
even jewelry breaks,
and precious stones are always lost or stolen—
but poems that show your beauty live forever.

I'm not ungenerous, but I hate to bid,
to fix a price,
or argue it away.

Next time you see me never speak of money:
nor think of it.
         Then, then, I'll give you love!

ELEGY XIII

TO AURORA

From deepest ocean floors, from the withered
    arms
of an ancient husband she has begun her flight.
Even now, her chariot wheels
turn white with frost,
her hair to fire,
and both are signals of the early hour,
the almost-morning. Aurora wait!

Why speed your flames across the colors of twi-
    light,
the fall of Memnon's ashes
fluttering like wings,

like gray bird wings
meeting in solemn battle across the sky?
Those very shadows hold the hour of love:
held lightly in her arms,
my love enfolds me.
Great treasure it is to know she is so near
through sleeping dark,
through cooling air to drift
toward bird song pouring from uplifted throats
that trill like rippling waters
in their music.
                    O Dawn-Aurora wait!
Why ride so soon, so near,
unwanted by flushed girls and waking lovers?
Quick with your rose-tipped fingers,
O Aurora,
pull short your chariot reins!
Before your race begins,
the wary pilot
still looks aloft and steers by beckoning stars,
but dawnlight leaves him floundering mid-ocean.
And as you rise,
the sleep-filled traveler
wearier than the road he walks starts on his way.
From where you ride, you are the first to see
the heavy soldier
adjust his iron gear with brutal hands,
to see the farmer
struggle against blind earth,
and you are first to call
the slow ox to his chores beneath the yoke.
Your wakening light
tricks the poor schoolboy from his love of sleep
back to his classroom and the teacher's whip.

And by your light
half of our crooked city
crowds into courts of law:
at one slip of the tongue the case is lost;
the client rages and the lawyer knows
another trial will lose more sleep tomorrow.

When you wake the city
you punish girls who drop their work at sunset;
you drag them to their places
at the loom.
Can I forgive you?
               I'm sure that others can't—
unless you find a monster who's indifferent
whenever his mistress leaves him
cold and lonely
to find her gone so early in the morning.
I've often wished you deep
in darkest midnight,
or that the stars outshine you through the skies.
I hoped the night would come
when black winds shattered
your chariot's axletree, your horses flying
blind through a fog, to slip, to fall mid-air!

Invidious Aurora!
             Why race through heavens
at your ungodly hour?
The warning was your son,
unhappy Memnon,
born black, the color of his mother's heart!
If Tithonus, your husband, had a voice,
O what a story
the old man could tell
complaining of young Cephalus and the like.
No wife in heaven
would have a darker blight!
Since Tithonus
is endless centuries old,
your flight from bed has wings—
age grows upon him (even Aurora feels
his hatred of her chariot in air).

But if sweet Cephalus held you in his arms,
you'd sigh, "Once more, my love,
my love, wait here,
drive deeper, wait, then ride—O swift night-
    horses!"

And if your husband is a fall of ruins,
it's strange unreason
to ruin my nights of love!
It is my fault you married an old man?

Think of the long, long nights that thoughtful
        Luna
reserved for her young lover,
Endymion—
and she was not less beautiful than you.
Jove never likes to see your face too often:
when he embraced Alcmene,
he made the night last twice as long as ours.

When I had done with scolding her, the Goddess
blushed till the sky turned red (of course, she
        heard me!). . . .
Day came no later than its usual hour.

ELEGY XIV

THE BURNING OF HER HAIR

How many times I've said:
"Stop pouring silver bleaches on your hair!"
No need to dye it now; it's almost gone.
My dear's a goose:
her hair was greatly rich: it fell below
her waist, her hips. My dear, your hair was
        perfect:
delicate to touch;
one feared to braid it—it was as fine as silk,
finer than silks that dark-skinned girls from Asia
wear at a feast,
and fragile as the spider's silver thread,
its colors dazzled, neither black nor gold,

of that rare light
that breaks through shadows of a spring-freshed
    valley,
and of the bark-stripped cedars on the hill.
And never twice the same;
it fell a hundred ways, in waves, in ripples,
nor comb's teeth tore it—
docile it was, and bright, and never angry,
so girls who dressed your hair need never fear it—
nor hairpin scratched their arms—
my girl as gentle as her cheerful hair.
So I have seen her of an early morning,
languid and naked,
serene as sunlight on her purple bed,
her hair in charmed disorder at one shoulder,
and she as lovely
as an escaped Bacchante down from Thrace,
fallen at ease within a green-wrapt forest.
Your locks of hair,
as soft, as innocent as fledgling feathers.
What trials, what terrors
their souls survived in heated forks and irons!
"Why singe, then torture them to death," I cried.
"Don't burn your head:
O iron-breasted girl, take pity on them—
why try to force them into waves and rings?
A wind-blown disarray
should be the best of beauty-making art!"
And now, they're gone,
burnt, scattered, poisoned—and their light, the
    crown
gay Bacchus and Apollo
would love to see upon their famous heads.
I saw a painting of the nude Dione,
sea-dripping goddess,
arms lifted up, her wave-washed hair like yours.
Why brood on ruins of ill-fated hair,
your looking glass
dropped from romantic, melancholy hands?
You saw a stranger's face glance from your
    mirror?

Forget what's past,
take your delight in what you are today.
No girl who envied you
deceived you with her aid to beauty secrets,
nor beauty parlor Madame with her magics
shipped in from Thessaly;
nor were you ill, nor evil eye pursued you.
The curse, my dear, was your own foolishness—
misfortune on your head!
Stripped German girls shall send you hair
    enough—
the riches of our conquered captive nations!
When someone stares at you,
at your false hair, I see your face turn red.
I know what's in your mind: "That fool's
    attracted
by a German female,
not me—a week ago, I'd show him hair that's
    mine!"
Red cheeks and tears are hidden by her right
    hand:
across her knees,
the charred remains of what she wore so gaily—
there like a gift sent to the wrong address.
My dear—no weeping!
The miracle will happen—not tomorrow—
but very soon—such glory grows again!
One early morning
The world will stop to say: "What marvelous
    hair!"

FROM AMORES

BOOK

II

TO A EUNUCH (1)

Hear me, Bagoas, janitor of wives,
the "the private eye"
that serves the jealous husband,
my words are few, but to the point: your
    mistress—
I saw her yesterday
(that radiant girl!)
where in the wake of Danaus' marble daughters
she strolled the porches of Apollo's temple.

I wrote at once to ask her for a date:
her trembling hand
replied, "Impossible!"
Then, "Why impossible?" I said. She answered,
You were to blame.

If you have brains, O perfect janitor!—
don't make me hate you:
men who breed fear are often killed or ruined!
Her husband is a fool,
if not why does he hire you to guard
the place that used to hold her maidenhead—
and now the maidenhead is nothingness,
a zero
he can neither lose nor find.
But since the man's insane,
go let him think
that girls who draw a crowd are always chaste.
Give her the freedom of the streets in town,
then you can take
your afternoons off duty,

an excellent exchange of liberties—
mistress and servant in conspiracy,
their secrets shared—if you're afraid of her,
pretend you're friendly
and the soul of honor.
Speak up for her: if she receives a letter,
then let your inner voice
say that her mother sent it. If a stranger
walks up to her,
say that you know him well, that he's her uncle.
Whenever she goes to visit her sick friend
(however gay he looks)
remember him as someone almost dead—
send him your blessings.

When she stays out all night, don't lose your
    sleep:
snore peacefully,
your head between your knees.
Ignore the rumors
of what she does when lost in Isis' temple,
or behind the columns of an amphitheater.

He who shares secrets
can turn his well-bred silences to gold—
is there an easier way
of making money?
Yourself (who is her friend)
will run her household—
all other servants crawling at your feet.
To hide the truth of how she spends her time
a million fancies flourish—
her husband hears
incredible romances—
even his orders wait his wife's consent.

After her husband frowns to show he's master,
he's ripe for lies
and loving blandishments—
she has her way.
Then let her rant against you, weep false tears,

let her complain
you'll be her worse-than-death,
that you accuse her
of crimes—of which she proves her innocence.

False charges make the simplest truths seem false:
accept her bribes,
and soon your well-earned riches
will buy your way to freedom from your masters.

Do you know why scandalmongers walk in
        chains?
And faithless hearts
are doomed to rot in swamp-filled prison cells?
Neck-deep in water, Tantalus yearns for water,
and fruit escapes
his nervous hands forever—
all this because of a loose tongue in his head.
Juno's slave, Argus, watchdog over Io,
came to an early death—
while Io was immortalized in heaven!

I've seen a beggar's legs shed blood in irons
because he told
a simple-minded husband
stories of how his wife enjoyed herself
naked in bed with friends,
even her brothers—
that filthy beggar's punishment was less
than what he should have earned:

                        the husband sad,
the girl restless and ruined.
A wife's disgrace is not for husband's ears:
if he's cold-blooded, he'll remain indifferent,
if hot,
your naughty stories will bring him grief.

However clear the case, proof of her guilt
is never as easy
as it seems to be:
The wife escapes the law,

the judge, her husband, restores his pride
by ruling in her favor.
Though he may catch her in the act, if she
denies it, then he'll call his eyes damned liars—
and if he sees her tears, he weeps aloud:
"Someone tells nasty stories
about my darling—
I'll see to it the bastard lands in jail."
Why play a game where odds are all against you?
And while you're whipped and beaten,
she's serene—
the happy wife perched on her husband's knee.

You need not fear us:
we have no thought of murder:
no knife in hand,
no poison in the wine—
live and let live—
and when she's in my arms, then let us love.
And for yourself, no trouble—
why should we ask for any more than this?

ELEGY III

TO A EUNUCH (2)

And all my agony because of you!—
monster who bars the way to her I love:
you're neither man nor woman,
a beast who's never known the joys of Venus!

Whoever was the first
to castrate boys
should have been clipped himself, his manhood
    gone.

If ever the heat of love
had waked your blood
perhaps you'd give way to a lover's prayers.

Nor born to ride a horse,
nor march a soldier,
you'll never wield a spear with your right hand—
in all your ways, no hope of manliness!
Your dress: a man's or woman's—
does it matter?
Your lady's colors are
all you may wear.
Her smile, your fortune—and your service, hers!—
and when she vanishes, where will you go?
Now she is ripe, her beauties fresh, yet warm—
a pity they should fade
through lack of love!
She can escape you any time she pleases.
(True lovers, she and I, shall find the way!)
We think it best
to try to beg your mercy (if you'll help us)
as long as you have favors left to give.

ELEGY IV

THE UNIVERSAL LOVER

This I admit: I'm very far from perfect.
I can't defend myself
with obvious lies—
if pleading guilty helps me, I'll confess—
say I've gone mad—then here's my list of crimes.
(I hate myself:

although I long to be what I am not—
if anyone got rid of all his sins,
he'd throw the greater part
of his weight away. I'm much too weak
to practice self-control: in storms mid-sea,
I'm like a boat that's rocked between the waves.

No single type of beauty is enough
to hold me fixed forever in her arms,
rather a hundred!
                    If the girl's modest
and, like a virgin, keeps her eyes downcast,
I turn to flames, her innocence my ruin.
Yet, if she makes advances,
I love a girl who's not a bashful kitten—
she gives me hopes at once
of half a dozen pretty tricks in bed!
Or if she stands aloof,
as cold and rigid as a Sabine matron,
then I suspect she waits on invitation,
eager to strip
and drop her strange disguise.
(Ladies, if you love study,
join me tonight
in adult education.
Or, if you're unrefined,
I'm sure to praise refreshed simplicities!)

And if some beauty
calls Callimachus' songs "provincial rubbish"
compared to mine,
and proves it while she's naked in my arms—
I love the girl, and like myself the better.
Or, if she plays the critic,
says I'm no poet, scolds my little verses,
I love to lure
such critics between the sheets,
and as I mount them, hear them moan and cry.

One girl
has feet as light as air—I love her footfall—

another walks as though her feet were lead,
yet she's the kind that turns
to melting softness
the moment that she feels the touch of love.
Because one beauty
sings a pretty song
and charms me with her sweet facility,
I'd love to try those lips at deep-drawn kisses.
And what of her
                              whose fingers stroke the harp
to wheedle music from the querulous string?
Who would not love such gifted, clever hands?
And still another
enraptures me with curves and turns in dancing—
herself is music when she takes the floor:
look at the quivering
of her hips and shoulders!
Since I'm susceptible to female rhythms,
I stand erect with all my blood on fire—
cold Hippolytus,
if he were in my skin, would be Priapus!

(And O blonde beauty,
tall as the daughters of our ancient heroes,
you fill the bed with love from head to foot—
yet I believe
a short girl, cute and naked, does as well—
for both destroy me—
I take them as they are, or great or small.)

If a girl's dowdy,
I dream of how she looks in décolleté,
and if she's smart,
she knows the art of showing off her beauty.
A girl with fair white skin and golden hair
turns to another
Venus in my arms—
she's my destruction—if her skin is dark,
I love a sun-tanned look—she's warm and easy,
yet if she's white as snow
with raven hair,

I'll not forget that Leda's hair was black—
or if it's auburn,
think of Aurora with her flaming curls!

My love would fit all heroines of history—
yet girls of ten or twelve
always attract me,
so does a matron who is ripe and eager:
one has experience—
and yet the others
charm me with promises of fresh delight.

Look, ladies, I am ready:
wherever girls are praised in this great city,
I'm there to hold them in my waiting arms!

ELEGY VI

CORINNA'S PARROT

Parrot, winged actor of the East, is dead:
come, birds of every color
to march in his cortege,
a flock of pious creatures at his funeral,
to beat your wings
against your throbbing breasts, to crook your
        claws
across your eyes, around your weeping bills:
nor tear your hair,
but pluck out all your feathers!
nor blow brass trumpets,
but sound the cry of mourning from each throat!
O ancient Philomena!
who wails against the tyrant Ismarus,

you've wept too long alone—
now tune your weeping cries for loss of Parrot,
the like of him will never talk again!
We know the fate of Itys
was murderous sad, and yet poor Itys died
too long ago—
now Philomena, weep new tears for Parrot.

May every bird who sails this hemisphere
cry grief and grief again,
and choose for our first mourner Turtledove.
Parrot and Turtledove!
Till Parrot's death, they found that life together
was like a song that never had an end!
They frolicked bird to bird
in love and friendship.
As youthful Phocis was to Greek Orestes
so Turtledove to you who was his hero:
as long as Fate permitted him that pleasure,
you were the living Parrot of his heart!
What can we hope or say
of friendships severed, of those charming colors
of throat and breast and wing,
and of your voice that was the perfect echo
of tears and laughter,
of shouts and cries?
How shall I soothe my girl who loved him well?
Unlucky Parrot
gone to that place from which no bird returns!

There was a flash of jasper
in your colors—
your crooked bill a flame of Punic fire!
Although your voice was often harsh and tuneless,
it had the charm of folk-song melodies.
Gross Fate who envies us
snatched you away.
                    You never went to war,
yet always brave,
a good, loud-talking lover of the peace.
(Look at these useless quails,

such birds forever quarreling with each other—
is it because they've reached the querulous age
of chattering wives?)

You were so delicate:
you talked so much you had no thought of meat.
You kept your diet:
stray nuts at dinner
with poppy seeds to bring deep dreams at night,
pure drops of water
were drink enough for you without the wine.

The Vulture lives, lives on,
so does the Kite who spirals through the air . . .
rain-maker Jackdaw lives . . .
so does the Raven (O how battle-dressed
Minerva hated him!)
live on as though he seems to live forever
(or so says rumor)
till nine full generations pass away . . .
yet our dear Parrot,
whose voice made noises like the sounds we make
(a priceless rarity, an Eastern treasure,
brought from the ends of earth)
gives up his ghost.
All that is best
is first fruit stolen by the hands of Fate:
all that is worst
seems to survive in glory of corruption.
Thersites lived to see
the funeral pyre of brave Protesilaus,
the first Greek killed at Troy;
after great Hector was a wraith of ashes,
his brothers flourished into middle age.

Why spend ourselves
in thankless bitterness
remembering prayers my lady spoke to save you?
She feared your early death—
and were her words lost in a South Wind
    tempest?

A seventh dawn came up—
which was your last—and there loomed Fate
     above you:
her distaff fallen,
yet with your dying tongue you called my
     mistress,
"Bless you, Corinna!"

Beneath a hill in far Elysium
a stately grove of dark-winged ilex stands
where watered grasses
grow forever green.
If we trust rumor,
that ground is hallowed by immortal birds.
(The wicked and obscene
must fly elsewhere)
This bourn the parking place
of gentle Swans, and there, unique and ageless,
the Phoenix burns!
Glittering for the delight in Juno's eyes,
the Peacock spreads his fan,
white Turtledoves rejoice in endless kissing.

Within the greenwood haven underhill,
the birds made way to welcome our good Parrot,
and all his pretty speeches
brought him praise.

His bones rest under
a rise of earth no greater than his body.
There, on his small headstone,
the sculptured words that everyone may read:
THIS MONUMENT SHOWS THAT MY MISTRESS LOVED
     ME:
MY LARYNX HAD GREATER WIT THAN ANY BIRD'S.

THE INNOCENT CRIMINAL

I'm on trial every day: is this to be
each day forever?
And you accuse me of another crime,
after you've charged me
with misdemeanors, felonies, and rapes!
Even if I win my case,
I'm sick of talk, of explanations,
endless arguments.

If, when we're at the theater, I turn round
to glance at marble galleries behind us,
then you insist
a woman's waiting for me—
so far away that she's invisible—
and yet she is the cause of your complaint.

Or if a quiet, handsome woman turns
merely to look at me,
you say her face reveals an invitation—
To what? To whom? To me!
To spend a month of nights with her in bed!

If I praise someone,
your hands leap toward me, tearing at my hair;
if I abuse the girl,
then you are certain
I keep her for unmentionable diversions.
If I look healthy,
I'm indifferent to you—
if I look pale, I yearn for other women!

I wish I knew whatever has gone wrong,
or how I've gone astray;
the convict when he stands before a judge
has earned his punishment
and keeps his poise.
But now you torture me with fantasies,
foolish ideas
of what you think I've done—
and you are angry—
you have no proof of anything at all!

Do you hope to drive me?
See that poor creature,
the long-eared, drooping ass, piled high with
      curses,
beaten and kicked and mauled
at every crossing
until the beast is almost motionless.

And still another judgment brought against me:
Cypassis thrown at me—
that artful, clever girl who does your hair—
and she and I
this very afternoon
left signs of making love between the sheets—
and in her lady's bed!
That girl's a slave!
When I step out for pleasure,
the Gods find me far better girls each night.
What man of taste
would care to take the girl
who when she's naked
shows that her back and buttocks love the whip?

It is her duty
to beautify your hair, to be your servant,
to make her brilliant hands move at your will—
and do you think
I'd compromise her loyalty?
For what? She'd laugh at me—and then betray me.

By blessed Venus,
by bows and arrows of her winged boy,
I condemn and then deny my latest crime!

ELEGY VIII

TO CYPASSIS

O Cypassis, creator of miracles,
fit handimaid for Gods and Goddesses,
an artist, if you please,
of the Greek coiffure
or the local hairdo in a thousand styles.
Yet you reserve for me a greater art,
not oversimplified, nor too elaborate—
those secret moments
of delight in bed!
Who found us naked when we played together,
and told Corinna?
Who knew the truth?
How did she know or guess?
Or did my face grow red, or did I stammer?
Nor did I drop a word of what we did!
And did I tell her
that one who slept with slaves
had dubious taste or else had gone insane?
Perhaps I did.
          Yet Cypassis, remember,
it was the beauty of his slavish Briseis
that fired Achilles:
captive Cassandra charmed great Agamemnon—
since I'm no greater than these famous heroes,
then who am I
to doubt the choice of kings?

But when Corinna in her lightning rages
turned flaming eyes on you,

your cheeks turned red.
If you recall, I kept my self-control!
I said, "By Venus, I love Corinna truly!"
(O Goddess Venus,
where the Aegean circles near Carphasus
may South Wind tempest in his darkest fury
drown all my pitiful lies
and blasphemies,
spoken as innocent words from my pure heart!)

Dear dark-skinned Cypassis,
Corinna did not
entirely disbelieve me:
think how I saved your waning reputation.

Lift up your skirt, for I shall mount you quickly—
Look I am ready!
And you say "No!" Ingratitude, my dear!
Are you afraid?
                        Come, that's a new excuse!
Your lady is my mistress; I'm your master:
if you say, "No!" again
I'll leave to tell her
your naughty tricks with men, how you've un-
        done me
even in her bedroom, eager and undressed—
and last, how many times we've come together!

ELEGY XI

CORINNA'S VOYAGE

When pines were felled at highest Pelion
these were the first
to make a ship that lured
mankind into his devilish routes at sea—
then through the gliding rocks
that crashed around her,

the ship that stole the Golden Fleece escaped!
even great waters spread their waves and
    marveled!

O how I wish the *Argo* had gone down
to drink the deeps of hell,
or since that wretched hour no one dared
to plunge swift oars through wild and foaming
    waters!

Look where Corinna wanders,
her welcome bed, her Household Gods deserted—
she's on her way to cross the angry waves.
Since I'm to stay at home
(Unhappy me!),
and there alone I'll dream of how she fears
the sullen weathers
of the shifting winds:
the West, the East, and then—without a warning—
the freezing North
attacks the humid South.

On that far voyage,
no cities welcome you (reckless Corinna!)
nor friendly trees, nor flowers from your garden,
only the farther distance into nowhere
above the endless movement of the waves.
In that great wilderness
of gliding waters
no one discovers
the frail sea shell and multicolored stones—
these are the treasures of our thirsty beaches:
so far the way is safe—and girls may loiter,
leaving the marble-white trace of their footsteps
on sea-swept sands.
Beyond that point toward sea, all routes are blind!

Let others speak of storms,
of raging waters
where Scylla and Charybdis pour their fury,
of rocks

where violent mountains loom above them,
or where the winding shores of Africa
wait for them
with deceiving reefs and caves.

If you have doubts, believe what others tell you:
better be credulous than lost at sea!

Even now, the hour's too late:
land fades behind you—
the cable slipt, the keel rides high and free.
The troubled sailor holds his fears in mind:
he trembles at the wind, and sees Death's face
stare up at him
from cold and shaking waters.

Then if old Triton strikes, he whips the waves:
and it is then you feel your lips turn white,
calling for rescue from the highborn stars,
the famous Gemini
of stormy skies,
the twins prolific Leda gave to heaven.

I hear you say, "O happy, happy she,
the girl who never leaves her native land!"

Wiser for you if you had overslept
the hour your boat leaped wildly from the shore—
or read, or let your fingers stroke the lyre.

If all my words (I hear the roaring winds!)
are blown away,
may Galatea smile upon your voyage.
Hear me, Nereus' Daughters,
even Granddaughters of your Godlike father—
it would be murder
if my Corinna, loveliest girl on earth,
perished at sea!

Then, as you go, Corinna, think of Ovid,
and may a lucky wind from distant skies

(swifter than one that takes you far away)
fill up the sails
that bring you home again.
Then may our great Nereus tilt the waters
in my direction
pouring high tides and winds against our shores—
and now, Corinna,
pray to Zephyrus,
for your own hands must shake the rigging free!

Soon as your famous ship
glides into harbor,
I shall be first to see it heave in view
with, "Hail to the blessed sails
that bring my Goddess—
as well as the Gods who carry her to shore!"

And you are in my arms—O what deep kisses!

There, on the beach,
a lamb for sacrifice:
the sands will serve us for both couch and table—
and then, the wine!
You'll tell me your adventures:
the ship almost went down—but speeding home
(because you thought of me)
you had no fears—
nor wild South winds, nor darkest night could
    scare you!

Let me believe the blushing lies you tell,
and why should I say "No" to flattery?
May Lucifer,
the topmost star in heaven,
gallop his horses till we meet again.

TRIUMPH OF LOVE

Crown me with laurels: here's a victory!
See me in glory:
Corinna rescued and my arms around her,
for she's escaped
her fatal enemies:
Dull Husband, Stupid Eunuch, and Locked Door,
the trio that held her fast because they feared
my sleight of hand:
no bloodstains anywhere—
the field was cleared at night: pure victory!
No walls have fallen,
nor cities burned, their harbors up in flames—
yet I'm Commander of a lovelier fortress,
a captivated girl!

When Troy had fallen in a ten-years' siege,
honors were handed out to many heroes—
what part of them
could Agamemnon claim?
My glory's all my own: no soldier shares it—
nor infantry, nor cavalry, nor cornet—
none other has the right
to all I've won.
My girl was not the first to start disruption:
if Tyndareus' daughter Helen had not been raped,
all Europe and Asia
would have slept in peace.
And a woman caused a foolish, drunken brawl
between the Lapith foresters and Centaurs.
On Latin ground
a second Troy took fire—

the call to arms roused Turnus and Aeneas—
again we found a woman
was behind it!
Young Rome fought over women in the streets,
a bitter Sabine scrimmage:
each father-in-law against each eager Roman.

O I have seen young bulls fall into battle
over an innocent-looking, milk-white
little cow
who stands aside—but cheers them on to fight!

Cupid, the Lord of many's my Chief of Staff:
in bloodless victory
I take his orders:
I wear his colors in every field of war!

ELEGY XV

THE RING

Hear me, O ring:
my pretty girl shall wear you on her finger!
yourself a Zero—
but your true value is the giver's love.
Go as my gift
to bring my lady pleasure,
circle her finger fair as she fits me
between her thighs when we are deep in love.
Twice lucky ring!
(Strange that a man should envy his own gift!
and yet I know how passionately, how sweetly
she'll stroke and tend it.)
Or rather, I would be that ring, transformed
by Circe's witchcraft or Protean arts
to grace her hand.

And now my love, my dear, open your tunic—
your hand to guide me where my touch discovers
your waiting breasts—and then, by lover's magic,
I'll escape your finger
and slip down to the haven of my delight.
(I'd help her seal love letters
in hopes her lips would meet me with a kiss.)
Nor would I let you
imprison me with jewels in a dark casket—
my gentle charms would make you fail to drop
    me.

Wear me each morning as we bathe together,
warm rain around us
as the fountains flow—
then see me brighten at your nakedness,
and though a ring,
I'll serve you like a man!
Why dwell on fantasies? My gift shall tell her
I'll love but her forever—

                go, little ring!

ELEGY XIX

THE TEMPTED LOVER

Sir—you're a fool!
Perhaps the wife you keep is faithful to you:
I doubt it—if the creature is a woman!—
then lock her up at home
to hide her from me.
If difficult to get, she's my fixation!
(The easy girl to meet invites neglect)
If she's aloof,
if someone says,
"Don't touch that priceless treasure,"

then my blood rises and I stir to action.
The man who takes the girl who's offered to him
has no more feeling
than an iron post.
True lovers live on dangerous hopes in fear,
on fears in hope:
near that abyss we raise a shrine to Love.

Why seek Good Fortune if she never fails us?
I never fall for love that leaves no scars!

Adroit Corinna found that weakness in me:
she has her way—she knows me all too well.
Often she says:
"Go home: I have a headache!
Don't drag your feet: get out: *please go away!*"
To hear her talk, she's Virtue on parade
(and when she's right, of course, I'm always
        wrong—
as far as blameless men
are ever guilty!)
Yet when my blood runs cool, she wakes its fires—
she's all for love: she's all my dreams and prayers.
O how she flatters me—and what sweet words!
Great Gods, how many kisses—
and what kisses!

And now, young lady,
since you're the latest girl to catch my eye,
beware of all my tricks
and promises,
and when I beg you to say, "Yes," say, "No!"
Then let me lie outside your bolted door,
awake throughout the long, frost-covered night.
So Love grows strong,
increasing with the years—
whatever starves my heat sustains its fires,
for Love that's overfed turns oversweet—
it palls the stomach—and we run away.

If Danaë'd not been locked in her brass tower

Jove never would
have made her what she became—
fashioned by him to be the perfect mother.
As long as Juno kept strict watch on Io
(even to change her to a cow with crumpled
     horns)
the girl looked like
a tempting feast to Jove!
The man who wants free lunches every day
must learn to diet on oak leaves and rain water.

But if a beauty wants to hold her lover,
she must outwit the man.
(This excellent advice is almost certain
to increase my troubles with the girls I know!)
I'm not a self-indulgent, lazy lover:
when girls advance, I'm sure to run away—
yet when they run,
I always follow after.

And you who seem indifferent to your girl
had better lock the door at sunset hour,
then turn to hear
soft footsteps down the hall—
ask why your dogs bark on a quiet night,
ask what is meant when messengers deliver
a letter to your wife
and speed the answer,
and most of all, inquire the mystic reasons
why she who is supposed to share your bed
prefers her own,
nor shares it with you more than once a week.

I hope anxiety eats away your bones!
Neglected wives
inspire me to action.
(Yet he who lures the wife of a damn fool
is like an idiot proud of cleverness
in stealing sand at night from empty beaches.)
My warning's clear:
if you don't lock her up, she's not my fancy.

O I've been patient:
I've waited for your anger and your pride
to test my wits, to show the world how well
I show a lover's skill
in my deceptions.
But you are dull, insensitive, and friendly—
you tolerate
what husbands can't abide—
damn your good nature that half-murders love!
O my misfortune!

               I meet her everywhere:
no terrors at midnight?
no naked girl who clings and fears revenge?
no tears and sighs and whispers in the dark?
and you do nothing
to make us wish you dead?

What shall I do with happy, easy husbands
who try to rent their wives or give them to me?
(This husband is the kind
who ruins our pleasure.)
Sir, look for someone else, someone who's willing
to wait six months
before you kick him out—
don't look to me—yet if you want my favors,
make home her prison, bar the bedroom door.

FROM AMORES

BOOK

III

LADY AT THE RACES

"Lady, I did not come to play the horses,
but let me hope
you've placed bets on the winner.
I'll sit beside you—there! Now let us talk;
subject: your beauty—
let me prove my case:
I'm deep in love and you're my inspiration!
The while I look at you,
you watch the races:
we're both entranced—our eyes are filled with joy.

"(Whoever he is, O happy Charioteer—
and does he ride your money, hopes, and fears?
Then let me take his place:
now, at the start,
I'll leap into the chariot, brave as he,
shouting my horses on from trot to gallop,
loosening the reins, my whip across their backs,
careening round the course
on tilted wheels!—
then, as I'll see you, sitting above the crowds,
the chariot halts,
and reins drop from my hands. . . .)
"O Hippodamia, when Pelops saw your face,
he was so dazed,
so absolutely dazzled,
he was almost murdered by a Pisacan spear
(which is how I am
when I look at you beside me)

83

yet he won the day by grace of his good lady—
that's how to win our races in love's name,
each lover
with his arms around his girl!

"Why shrink from me?
                              How can I move away?
We have no choice: the painted lines beneath us
show how we sit in rows,
each touching each, our arms, our hips together—
a close design of seating in the Circus!
" 'But you, Sir, to our right,
give her more room!
You'll crush her ribs!
                              And you behind her,
draw in your legs (if you're a gentleman!)
before you break her back against your knees!' "

"Look down, my dear, your stole,
your wrap has slipped:
it sweeps the floor—catch it. . . . I'll pick it up!
I envy it. It covers loveliness.
O what one sees in draping it around you!

"What priceless legs, my dear—like Atalanta's
that Milanion's hands
reached out to capture!
Your thighs one sees in painting of Diana,
stripped for the hunt,
herself as brave and reckless
as the wild creatures of the woods around her.
My blood was up before I saw your treasures—
what shall I do?
                              Am I to live in flames,
add fire to fires and water to the sea?
Under your tunic, scarcely out of sight,
I think I know the rest—what joy, what rapture!

"Now, as we wait, shall I
make breezes blow?
and stir them with a fan to start them flowing?

Perhaps this wave of heat
pours from my heart—
and not the air around us, but my breast—
that burns with love
to find such beauty near!
Even as I talk a rain of dust has fallen
on your thin tunic—there! Away with it!
What horrid dust to stain that snow-bright skin!

"Here's the parade:
all at attention—quiet!
Now you may cheer—the golden Gods are
        coming—
all images of heaven on parade:
First Victory in glittering wing-spread flight—
please make my love's swift horse
an easy winner!

"Let those who risk their lives
on treacherous waters
cheer Neptune—but the sea is not for me!
I'd rather keep
my footing on the shore.
Let soldiers shout for Mars—but I hate fighting:
I welcome Peace, and where Peace builds her nest
I always find delight
in making love.
Let Phoebus lead his oracles and prophets,
and Phoebe guide the hunter to his quarry.
I'd like to see
Minerva turn and bow
while all her craftsmen clap artistic hands!
Let rural gentry rise to welcome Ceres
and sing their praise
for gay, soft-natured Bacchus!
While prize-ring fighters stamp the ground for
        Pollux,
hard-riding horsemen
worship Castor's skill!
But we have saved our cheers: 'Sing loud for
        Venus!'

for she's our Goddess,
and cheer again her naughty, naked boys.
And when I meet a girl like this new lady,
smile on me, Venus—fold her in my arms!
Great Venus nodded—
that means all is well:
if Venus makes a promise, it's your duty
to make the promise and the wish come true—
then love me sweetly—
you're the Greater Goddess!
By all the witnesses we have around us,
by all the Gods who passed us on parade,
come, be my mistress,
keep my heart forever—
and I'm your servant, till the end of time!

"But look, my dear,
your feet are off the floor—
sit back securely while I lift them up
to place them tiptoe on the iron railing.

"At last the track is cleared:
and four-horse chariots at the starting line:
I've found the jockey who has caught your eye—
if you've inspired him,
his race is won,
even his horses know your heart is with them!
But O, good grief! he's rolling wild and wide—
has he gone crazy?
Look, the one behind him
is near, gains at a gallop—steams ahead!
That Charioteer is out to ruin my girl,
to kill her hopes,
to throw away her money. . . .
Pull up the left reins, Fool,
you'll wreck the chariot, Stupid!
My dear, your bets are on an ignoramus!

"Romans, call off the race. Toss out your togas!
Then dive beneath my cloak,
if togas fly,

they'll strangle you or devastate your hair.

"See how they start again—the gates swing open—
they're off with colors streaming round the
     track—
and here's the last chance
for your Charioteer—
and he's ahead—look how he's riding in.
Well done, my man, for you have saved my lady!
Your Charioteer rides up
to take his palms—
but what of mine that you must give to me?"
She smiled—I saw her eyes light up with promise—
of what? I cannot tell—and yet I know:
I smiled and said:
"Enough, my love, not here, some other place,
we'll play et cetera both day and night!"

ELEGY III

LADY IS A LIAR

Don't lose faith in the Gods—
they are still in heaven—
it was my thoughtless girl who spoke their names:
she swore by Jove, by Venus—
then broke her promise—
and yet her lovely face is still unchanged!:
her hair magnificently long
as ever,
as though the Gods had never been betrayed—
her skin the color of light
at half-past noon,

her cheeks the red of roses found in snow,
her feet as delicate
as works of art,
and she as tall, as beautiful as before!
As ever her eyes are bright as new-lit stars
to tell me lies,
more lies—and still more lies!
(Truly enough, the Gods forgive a girl
who seldom tells the truth—
the gift of beauty
has rights which always make her seem divine!)
Not long ago, she took a solemn oath
and swore by her two eyes
as well as mine:
my eyes are blighted (Heaven takes revenge!)
while hers are brilliant as the light of day.
Tell me, O Gods,
why non-truth-telling, sinuous young females
walk fancy-free
while I must take the blame?
Do you remember sweet Andromache,
the girl sent down to death because her mother
possessed a fatal beauty?
                              Was that just?
Don't make the same mistake—think of my
      troubles:
I've proved the naughty girl
has formed the habit
of taking names in vain, or yours or mine—
which is as if
she's laughing at the Gods—
and I'm made victim of a perfect liar—
she works in crime: I get the punishment.

Either the name of God is meaningless,
to be feared by fools alone
to keep them faithful,
or if there is a God, his Godlike nature
is one that falls in love with frail young women—
and they alone do anything they please!

But as for men:
                Mars buckles on his sword,
a deadly spear flies from Minerva's hand,
Apollo draws the bow—and men are targets.
Forked lightning falls on us
and we're struck down
in fire and fury straight from Jove's right arm!

Although they know that women breed disaster
and disrespect for heavenly intentions,
the Gods grow timid
when a pretty girl
smiles all her sins away and shows no fear.

Why waste our piety at the smoking altar?
Men, what we need are men, and manly spirit!

When Jove pours lightning through his sacred
      forests,
he spares the females in the congregation—
these girls are so complacent,
they're a scandal—
of these, only poor Semele was hurt:
the girl was hot and terribly excited,
and when Jove pierced her, she went up in
      flames—
yet had she run away
from that Great Lover,
Bacchus himself would not enjoy the honor
of being son of Jove
(who nourished him
in his broad thigh and loved him like a mother).

Why do I trouble heaven with complaints?
The Gods have eyes,
kind hearts, and human feelings.
And were I God, some pretty little chit
who never told the truth would not unman me:
I'd say she was as loyal
as any woman,
that there are times when women speak the truth!

I'd never be ungallant
or severe.

And now, my dear, enough! Don't go too far:
don't take my name in vain, then lie to heaven!
And never, *never*, NEVER,
say your permission's granted by my eyes.

ELEGY V

THE DREAM

That night I fell asleep as if forever—
and then the terrors came
to haunt my soul:
below a sun-struck hill I saw a thicket
of ilex boughs that hid a million birds,
next to that place
a grassy knee-deep meadow
where springs of water made their silver music.
To escape the pouring heat
I neared the ilex
and sought out shelter under black-browed
        branches,
yet everywhere I stepped,
the heat rained down—
but look! across the broad and blossomed meadow
to feed on watercresses and crisp flowers
a white cow grazed—
I saw her whiteness
turn bright as snow before it melts away
to join in streams of sunlit, flashing water,
brighter than milk
that steams and foams in whiteness

until the udders of the ewe run dry.

A bull had joined the cow, and like a lover
he lay beside her in the grassy meadow.
And as he stayed there,
ruminating slowly,
tasting a second time rich herbs and cresses,
it seemed that sleep had drained him of the power
to lift his head:
his weighted horns seemed rooted in deep turf.

Then lightly, as though drifting down the air,
came that quick bird of night,
a deadly crow,
chattering through the grasses at his feet:
three times its beak
tore at the white cow's breast
and carried off a feast of snow-bright fur.
A black and blood-red wound below her neck,
the young cow turned away
to graze elsewhere,
then seeing bulls at play across the pasture,
she ran to meet them,
to share their riches in a greener haven.

"Tell me, soothsayer,
dread analyst of dreams and midnight fancies,"
said I, "what were these scenes that filled my
        eyes—
is Truth behind them?"
The man took gravely every word I said,
then he replied,
"The heat you tried to cool while shuddering
        leaves
branched overhead, yet you could not escape it,
was love's heat in your blood,
and the fair cow
was your blonde lady, naked at your side,
yourself the helpless bull who slept beside her.
The crow was some old witch who tapped her
        heart:

and then the white cow
slowly left her lover
which means you'll have a cold and lonely bed.
The black scars on her breast,
are clear enough—
they show the necklace worn by faithless
    women."
The soothsayer was done:
the air was chilled,
blood left my face, and Night stared in my eyes.

ELEGY X

HOMAGE TO CERES

Summer is ripe and it is Ceres' season:
these nights
my girl tarries in bed alone.
O Ceres of the golden hair and crown,
trimmed with the blossoming wheat
and shining fair,
why torture lovers with your celebrations
that turn to sadness
while they sleep apart?

In every land we know your generous giving:
wherever men have cause
to count their blessings,
no Goddess shows less malice toward mankind.

Before you tended earth, the goatskinned farmer
lived on stray herbs,
moist cresses, fallen acorns,

the fruit of Jove's oak where one heard dark
    omens.

You taught the peasant
how to thresh his grain.
Ceres it was who urged the seed to grow,
the scythe to move
among the glittering corn,
the ox to shoulder burdens at the plough,
plough's crooked tooth
to furrow ancient soil.

Does this same Goddess welcome lovers' tears
and smile at rules
that force unhappy lovers
to leave their girls and lie awake till morning?
However well she tends
her fields and gardens,
Ceres is not a senseless country wife;
she knows the power of love—she has a heart.
I'll call the Cretans in
to prove my case—
on some occasions Cretans tell the truth!

Crete had the privilege of nursing Jove,
in Cretan pastures
the power that rules the world and stars above us
was once a child
whose infant lips drank milk with native
    children.
Therefore
we have great faith in all their legends—
even Jove believes them:
Ceres herself won't question or deny
a charge of moral turpitude against her—
the story of
her love affair in Crete.
Under Mount Ida—there she saw Iasius,
his spear was held erect
with steady hand,
and then she saw it flash—the beast run through—

herself was pierced—
she blushed at what she felt—then fire took her,
she shook with shame and love
from head to foot.
And yet love conquered.

Rich earth had turned to dust and the grain
        withered—
our clever tools,
even the plough? were useless—
on sun-baked clay, seeds scattered to the wind:
with all their prayers unheard,
peasant and farmer
felt lost and cheated and despaired of heaven.

Meanwhile, our Goddess of fertility
deep in green forest
spent days and weeks and months in making love
on beds of fern—a rapturous siesta!
The golden crown of wheat
fell from her hair. . . .
Only in Crete
the changing year grew fruitful through the
        seasons—
wherever Ceres
gave herself to love
the very wilderness turned warm and fertile.
Mount Ida, once a waste
of brush and briar
changed to broad fields
of shining oats and barley—
a flashing harvest reaped by the wild boar.
King Minos hoped such luck would last forever.

O golden Goddess:
if sleeping all alone made you unhappy,
why bring me grief throughout your holidays?
Why make me dull and sad?
                        Your trials are over:
Young Proserpina is no longer lost;

she is chief mistress of a mighty kingdom—
only Queen Juno,
up among the clouds,
can say she rules a livelier world than hers.

Ceres, the proper tribute to your name
should speak your praise
with love and song and wine—
love-making at a feast, sunset to morning—
these are the priceless gifts of men to Gods.

FROM   THE ART OF LOVE

You who are green recruits at making love
First find the girl; the next step is to take her—
And third—to make your love a long embrace.
These are my teachings and the ground I cover—
My chariot speeding round the course that wins.

While you are free, and riding as you will,
Reins loose at fingertips, be very careful
To whom you say: "It's you alone for me!"
The perfect girl—a sight for weary eyes—
Won't drop from heaven, gliding at your side.
You shall have to seek her out.

                                   The hunter knows
The place to trap the deer and in which covert
The wild boar grinds his teeth or wakes or sleeps
He knows where game is caught, or reeds or
        grasses,
And he who baits his hook knows fishing waters.
So you, who're out to know the ways of love,
To find the right girl and to hold her straightly,
Seek out the places where young females wander—
Nor shall I set your sails before the wind,
Nor send you roundabout on a long road.
Though Perseus found his dark-skinned Androm-
        eda
In western Asia and a Trojan lover
Invaded Greece to steal a Grecian girl,
In Rome you have the choice of countless
        darlings:
"Here," you can say, "the girls are everywhere,
The best of hand-picked beauties in the world!"
They grow like grain that covers half Mount Ida,
As many girls as grapes in Lesbos vineyards,
Birds in the trees, or fishes in the sea,
Or stars that fill the midnight vaults of heaven—
Where girls are many—that's your native Rome
Where Venus lives, true Mother of Aeneas.

Do you like them in their young and slender years,
Teen-aged and fresh? She stands before your
    eyes!
Or do you want them ripe, full-bloomed, and
    ready?
A thousand wait for you! At times it's difficult
To make your choice. Perhaps you like them
    older,
Adroit and matronly, more dignified,—
These, let me tell you, run to many thousands!
On afternoons when sunlight falls upon us
In gold, the hair of Hercules' great Lion,
Stroll at your ease in Pompey's Portico,
Or walk in shade beneath the marble columns
A mother raised in memory of Marcellus,
Her famous son. And don't neglect the shelter
Of Livia's porches where antiquities
Of painted art keep Livia's name alive—
And don't forget the temple of Apollo
Where granddaughters of Belus stand in stone
Death in their minds forever plotting murder
Of helpless cousins they were forced to marry;
Their father faces them with naked sword.

Don't let the holidays escape your notice,
The day that Venus weeps for her Adonis
And girls are eager to receive a lover,
Nor the seventh day each week, the day of rest
Of Jews from Syria, nor Io's temple,
Where many a virgin learns to take on men
In the same way that Io welcomed Jove.
Even the courts of law (though who would think
    it?)
Are often thoroughfares that lead to love.
Love's flames take fire in passionate dispute
For Venus has her altar in the Forum
And bright Appian fountains spurt in air—
The place where lawyers are outtricked by Love,
Where he, defending others, trips himself,

The agile talker dumb—while a new case
Is placed before the court, his own defeated.
So Venus laughs at legal rights gone wrong,
And lawyers envy many a careless lover. •

But most of all search through the amphitheaters;
These places answer all your hopeful prayers:
They come in droves: women and girls are there,
Yielding against the wall, or grave or playful—
So you may taste her or decide to keep her
As ants in narrow lanes and long, long queues
Move past each other, carrying wheat or corn,
As bees at pasture hover over flowers
And float above the thyme, so stylish women,
Free for an afternoon, crowd to the circus—
So bright, so many, even my judgment fails.
To see the show, they come to show themselves
And chastity is lost in half an hour.

You, Romulus, were first to use the circus
For pleasures of this kind—that was the day
When Sabine women gratified new husbands.
Nor roof nor curtains covered marble walls
And there, down front, no flaming yellow
     crocus—
Merely a twisted wreath of leaves and vines
Grown on the Palatine, an artless stage,
No seats but mounds of grass where people sat
To shade their eyes, leaves covered unwashed
     hair.
•The men look round them, measuring each girl
As though each one contained his heart's desire.
Tuned to the squealing of a Tuscan flute
A dancer tapped the floor in treble beat,
And then among the cries of wild applause
(Those days applause was always unrefined),
King Romulus gave the signal: *Take the women.*
The men leaped shouting at the girls before them
And mounted them with savage, tearing hands.
The girls turned white as timid turtledoves

Attacked by eagles, and as white as lambs
Who see a wolf—and all were terrified—
Each in a different way, fear made them one:
Some tore their hair while others looked insane;
Some sat bewildered; others screamed for mother;
One had no voice at all; another wept;
While one stood still, another ran away;
As girls were mounted, they began to yield,
Even their fears increased their melting pleasures.
And if a girl resisted a new lover
Who carried her up, against his passionate breast,
He'd say, "Why ruin those soft eyes with tears?
I'm as your father was to your own mother;
Like him, I'll do the very same for you!"
O Romulus, of all our kings and rulers,
You, you alone knew how to pay your soldiers:
Give me such riches and I'll join the service.
A Romulus tradition in our theaters
Is proof enough that women love disaster.

In making love remember tears have power,
For tears move iron; let her see them fall,
Or if your cheeks are dry (tears sometimes fail),
Moisten your eyes with fingers dipped in water.
Who kisses her at all—if he is wise—
Without a tempting whisper of soft words?
She may refuse the kind of kiss you give her
But kiss her as you will—at first she may
Attempt to fight, and say, "Impossible;
You're very naughty," yet the girl is ready
To lose herself in glorious defeat.
But as you take her lips, don't make them bleed—
Don't let her say that you're uncivilized.
Yet he who takes his fill of yielded kisses
And does not take her, naked and complete,
Deserves to lose the little that he won.
Then what are kisses for? To make her cold?
You had a fit of rural diffidence—
Or did you think her Virtue in Distress?

Women like action with a show of power.
They love to give their best unwillingly.
And she who yields to sudden violence—
One good bold stroke and she is overcome—
Believes her charms are irresistible.
Yet she who might have yielded if hard-pressed
Puts on a cheerful mask to say good-bye—
She feels neglected and a little sad.
Phoebe was mounted at one blow, so was her
     sister;
And both girls loved the boys who took them
     bravely.
And there's the famous case of Deidamia
Who had the bright Achilles for a lover:
The time was after Venus at Mount Ida
Was praised beyond two goddesses beside her,
And she rewarded Paris for his favor
By helping him with Helen, that Greek girl,
Now safely wifed behind the walls of Troy—
The daughter-in-law of Priam from far shores.
Meanwhile the Greeks were loyal to Menelaus—
His private grief become a public cause.

Turned to a coward by his mother's fears,
Achilles dressed himself in girlish clothes.
What is this nonsense, son of Aeacides?
The art of spinning wool is not your talent;
Pallas has arts of war to build your fame:
And baskets on your arm? Go, wear a shield—
Why hold a skein of wool in your right hand,
Your hand that is the very death of Hector?
And throw away the endless-winding spindle!
Your hand is made to thrust the Peleian spear!
He shared a bed with Princess Deidamia
And when he entered her, she found a man.
No doubt the girl was raped, yet being raped
Was something she desired. When he left her,
She cried, "Once more, once more, don't go
     away—"

He had dropped the spindle and displayed his
    sword.
Why should he force you now, O Deidamia;
Why tempt him with soft words, why make him
    stay?
Just as one has a little touch of shame
As one begins to yield, so there's delight
At yielding to his love and all your pleasure.

Good-looking lovers, fortunate and easy,
Should never wait for her to make advances:
The man is first to act; he pleads, he begs;
While she begins to melt with flattery.
If you would take her, speak; she waits to hear
    you;
Give her excuse to get what you enjoy.
When Jove went out to meet his famous beauties
He fell upon his knees; no girl seduced him.
But if your pleading swells her vanity,
Stay where you are; step back in quick retreat,
For many girls prefer elusive tactics;
They don't like eagerness—check your advances,
Nor let them weary at the sight of you.
Nor let your hopes of meeting them in bed
Become sole topic of your conversation:
Let Love take what he wills in Friendship's name.
O I have seen a most unwilling beauty
Accept a friend who soon became her lover.

Women have hearts so various and strange,
One learns a thousand ways of making love.
No stretch of land is best for every harvest:
Here vines are grown, and over there, rich olives,
And still another, marvelous in wheat.
The heart takes on disguises out of air,
As many shapes as this wide world contains;
Wise lovers wear a mask for each occasion:
Like Proteus, one is volatile as water,

Or is a lion, or deep-rooted tree,
And then a wild-haired boar. Fish may be caught
In many different ways: some with a spear,
Others with hooks, and many are hauled in
Dragged to the boat in huge cave-bellied nets.
No one technique serves women of all ages:
The full-grown deer is not a careless doe—
She looks before she leaps, the trap unsprung.
Don't boast of learning to dim-witted females;
Or show off wit to shy, suburban matrons
You'll make them feel inferior and stupid—
Some women often fear an honest lover,
Yet always feel at ease with clever liars.

FROM *THE ART OF LOVE*

Book II

If you would keep a lady at your side
Make sure she thinks her beauty holds you fast:
If she wears purple, praise her purple dress;
Or white, say she looks lovelier than ever;
Or gold? Tell her that she herself enhances
The worth of gold; or homespun tweeds, why
     then
Speak of good taste, and all her charms concealed;
Or if undressed, half naked in her shift,
She stands before you, waiting for applause,
Say, "O my dear, you've turned my blood to
     fire!"
Then whisper gently, "Darling, you'll catch cold."
If she has wind-blown hair, then parts it straightly,
Tell her how smart she looks, or if she curls it,
Say that her hair improves the arts of nature.
And when she dances, say her arms are lovely,

And O her voice is perfect when she sings—
Your grief is that her songs can't last forever.

• And when you meet her naked in your bed
Where everything is joy, her arms around you—
Then let her know the glories of the night.
Even if she's violent as fierce Medusa,
She melts with joy when she receives her lover.
Yet as you talk to her, make sure your voice
Seems steady and sincere; don't let your eyes
Destroy the magic of well-chosen words.
True art conceals itself, and if discovered
Is an embarrassment and shows a liar,
A fool who'll never learn to be a lover. •

Though autumn seems to be a glorious season,
The grape flushed with its promise of red wine,
The days are bright: one day we're stiff with
    cold—
The next, we melt away in sudden heat—
The changing climate leaves us weak and drowsy.
I hope your lady's well—if dubious skies
Find her beneath the weather, feverish and limp,
Then show the girl you love her. That's the time
Daily affection sows a future harvest.
Don't let her illness make you seem impatient—
Your hands are there to stroke her as she wills:
Give her pale lips a multitude of kisses,
And let her drink your sympathetic tears.
Promise her everything—and more against the
    future:
To disinfect her room, bring an old woman
To give her eggs, change sheets, and light up
    sulfur—
This shows your thoughtfulness, a bland tech-
    nique
To make her happy to your own advantage.
And as you wait on her, don't go too far;
Do nothing that displeases: don't dictate

Her diet or the drinks that she refuses—
These horrid tasks are left to scolding nurses,
To clumsy husbands and defeated rivals.

The wind that fills your sails at leaving shore
Is not the same that drives them through mid-seas.
•While young let love go roving as it wills
To learn its manhood and to gain its way:
O feed it well—it will be strong enough.
The very bull that makes a mortal tremble
Was once a calf you led and stroked its ears:
And where you rest the tree that leans above you
Was once a pale green fluttering shoot of leaves:
Each river at its source seems thin or shallow,
Yet as it flows downstream, it gathers power,
Winding and roaring with its many waters. •

Make sure your lady knows and needs your
     favors—
Nothing is more important till she knows you—
Till that is done, no signs of weariness.
For she must always see you, hear your voice,
Or night or day your face must be her vision.
When you are sure that she would hate to lose you
Then disappear; perhaps she needs a rest:
The field lies fallow for a future season—
Dry earth drinks down deep draughts of heaven's
     rain.
When Demophoön was near, his looks and actions
Warmed Phyllis with love's heat, yet when he
     vanished—
For he had sailed away—she was all fire.
While shrewd Ulysses stayed away from home,
Penelope was tortured day by day—
(O Laodamia, Protesilaus
Had also vanished, leaving you alone.)
Brief absences are best: a long retreat
Means that love pales, grows thin, then disappears,
And new love enters. While her Menelaus
Stepped out of sight, brave Helen had her way—
For she was never made to lie alone—

And shared her nights with an engaging guest
Who when he held her close would keep her
     warm.
What is this nonsense, husband Menelaus?
While you walk off alone, your wife, her guest
Are left to sleep together in one bed.
Are you insane? Do you encourage hawks
To stand guard over doves? Or mountain wolves
To tend a herd of sheep? Helen's not guilty,
Nor is her lover wrong: he does what you,
What any man would do on that occasion:
The time, the place are there—and you are gone!
You made them go to bed; the girl was quick
To take the hint you gave her. What was she
To do? her husband gone—and here's a guest
Who is no fool, and in the room behind them—
What she fears most—a cold and empty bed.
O Menelaus, look! I pardon Helen:
She took the kindness of her friendly lover!

Don't ask a woman's age, or try to guess
Who ruled the state the hour that she was born:
These questions come from gray-faced bureau-
     crats,
Especially so if she is not too young,
If her first flowers are cut and first white hairs
Torn from her head, or artfully concealed.
These later years are rich, O restless lovers!
These fields yield fruit and you must sow them
     straightly
While you are quick and strong. Too soon, too
     soon,
Crook'd-back Old Age walks in on silent feet.
Bend to your oars, or plough the rugged earth,
Or use your fists in tight and bloody battle,
Or mount the girls to make them ask for more—
A warlike test of all your manly powers.
For women know their trade extremely well;
And years of practice make their practice perfect:

Time's loss is turned to gain—their artfulness
Shows never a sign of age—it seems eternal.
However you wish to tune them to your pleasure,
They'll answer in a thousand girlish ways—
No picture paints the methods they employ,
Women have more inventiveness than art.
Women who take you scarcely need temptation:
They love the give and take and yet once more
In bed joined with a man—yet men and women
Should take an equal measure of delight.
I hate to compromise, to take half-kisses—
That's why I lack a yearning for young boys.
I also hate the girl who goes halfway,
Who when she yields thinks that she's spinning
     wool.
• Never mix housework with my joys of love:
I loathe a woman who finds love her duty;
I want to hear her murmuring delights,
Her wordless cries, and "Hold me, stay awhile";
To see her drunk with love, her eyes enraptured,
Or see her drowsy, waiting to be waked,
Yet holding off the moment when she yields. •

After a woman passes thirty-five,
Her gifts are ripe, for Nature has endowed her
With skills unknown to girls of seventeen.
Let the impatient drink the new-made wine;
I'll take deep draughts from rich and well-stocked
     cellars.
Only the full-grown plane tree tempers heat
And shields us from the furies of Apollo—
And fresh-sprung reeds tear at our naked feet.
Would you take Hermione 'stead of Helen?
Is Gorge better looking than her mother?
If you desire beauties at their best,
Seasoned and ripe, and show yourself a man,
Your victories are those of love in glory.
You need not fear to win your just rewards.

Look at that broad sophisticated bed
Where willing lovers lie. Stand guard, my Muse,

Behind the closing door; you need not help them:
They'll speak well for themselves—their hands,
    their fingers
Will search out places where Love plants his
    arrows—
So Hector's hands pleased his Andromache,
Adroit in bed as they were skilled at war—
And so the great Achilles' as he fondled
Slave Briseis when he dropped, weary with fight-
    ing,
In her soft bed—his very hands stained red
With Trojan blood. (Was this your pleasure,
    Briseis,
To know his hand between your yielding thighs?
The naughty girl was happier than ever.)
O love's delight must not be reached too soon,
But warmed by fond delays. When you have
    touched
That place where women love to be consoled,
Don't be ashamed to stroke it as she wills,
Her eyes as bright as sunlight on clear waters.
Then she'll begin to murmur her soft cries,
Sigh gently, and find words that answer joy.
Don't fill your sail too high, and leave her waiting,
Nor let her speed ahead, keep pace together;
The full delight complete: then man and woman
Spent with their love, drop from each other's
    arms.
The slow pace is the best when you are free
To play and kiss and then begin again:
No fears to haunt the secret work of love.
But when both time and place are not your own,
And both precarious, bend to your stroke,
All speed ahead, and spur her flanks to motion
As galloping horses racing to desire.

FROM *THE ART OF LOVE*

Book III

Here I teach women how to act in love:
True women never march in battle gear
Nor carry torches or wild bows and arrows
(Few men I've seen are injured by these weapons;
Women have other means). Yet men betray,
And young girls almost never—if you ask,
You'll find them seldom charged with major
frauds.
After he gave her children, faithless Jason
Dismissed Medea, and took on another,
A bright young bride to warm his heartless.
breast.
So far as Theseus cared, poor Ariadne
Was food for sea gulls on deserted shores.
The beach where Demophoön had sailed away
Is called Nine Ways to mark the many times
That Phyllis ran to seek her vanished lover—
Listen! The very forest drops its leaves
And weeps aloud for drear, neglected Phyllis.
(Dido! Your guest, famous for piety,
The young Aeneas—even he betrayed you—
Gave you good cause—the sword of your destruc-
tion.)
Shall I tell you ladies how you fell to ruin?
You lacked the art of love. It's art, my dears,
That makes the act of loving live forever.
I hope that girls today learn art endures!
Queen Venus came before me in a vision
To say young females needed my instructions,

Then said: "Look at the miserable darlings,
Poor naked girls betrayed by full-armed men: •
Two poems show the way to their defense—
By Stesichorus—one had libeled Helen;
The second, written in a happier vein,
Sang out her praises on a golden lyre.
"And if I know you well," said smiling Venus,
"You'll be forever falling at their feet."
These were her words. She broke a spray of
    myrtle
(Worn as a wreath to bind her lovely hair)
And gave it me with two or three ripe berries,
Which, as I took them, filled me with such power
I saw the perfect light of radiant heaven—
And O my heart swept clear of all its weight!
Now, while Queen Venus is my inspiration,
Take my advice. I speak, of course, to girls
Who are old enough to love, to act as women,
To go their own sweet ways as women should.

•Don't load your earrings with crude stones of
    flashing colors—
That polycolored Indians wear for show—
The kind of jewel that's snatched from greenish
    waters;
Nor weight your dress with gilded ornaments,
Or lace of gold—such signs of lavishness
In golden nets to trap us, hurt our eyes.
We're captured by an artful elegance.
And don't neglect your hair: one touch of art
'll change your disarray to matchless beauty.
Nor is one style the best for all fair creatures—
Each girl should find her own and gaze devoutly
At what she sees in her own looking glass!
Her face is oval: straightly parted hair
(No ornaments at all) becomes her best—
This fashion was the choice of Laodamia.
Her face is round: then she should show her ears
And knot her hair up high upon her head.

One girl should let her hair drop to both shoul-
    ders—
The way Apollo looked when lost in music
And his deft fingers stroked the golden lyre.
Another girl should wear a braided crown
Such as Diana wore when she was dressed
Short-skirted for the hunt, waking the terror
Of beasts who ran before her.
                    This young beauty
Should let her hair fall loose—while yet another
Should wind her hair close to her shapely head;
One girl should wear a glittering tortoise shell,
Another, comb her hair in waterfalls.
Count all the acorns of the thick-boughed oak,
Count all the bees that swarm in Sicily,
Count all the savage beasts in Alpine forests,
Yet more than these are ways to dress your hair,
And each new day invents another fashion.
Wild wind-blown styles are often most attractive,
As though the girl had just stepped out of bed,
(And yet she came fresh from a beauty parlor)—
Art often imitates the casual air. •
The careless style was famous with Iole
(Who looked disheveled in a fallen city)
Whose air charmed Hercules. He said, "God help
    me;
This is the girl I love!" So Ariadne
In her distress looked wild and Bacchus raised her
Into his chariot to mount the skies,
While all the happy Satyrs danced and cheered!
Nature is kind to all of you, my dears,
She hints at many ways to hide your flaws.
Though Time strips all of us—hair falls away
As leaves before the wind. A woman tints
Her thin and fading crown with golden washes,
Her hair is then more glorious than ever.
Or she can walk out in a Transformation,
Piled high in golden braids upon her head,
And no one thinks the less of her for that!
Even in the Circus, on a crowded morning,
Where marble Hercules and the Nine Muses

Watch everything we do, the ladies buy
New curls or anything their heads desire.

●What shall I say of clothes and how to dress?
Gold lace is not my style, nor heavy colors;
I speak for lighter colors and few clothes,
The inexpensive dress that walks the street.
Don't go insane with diamonds and silks
Or try to wear a fortune on your back!
On days when South Wind brings no threat of
    rain
Look at the cloudless colors of the sky,
Wear these for love, or light, gold-tinted gray,
The color of the Ram (who, so I've heard,
Saved Helle and Phrixus from their shrewd step-
    mother).
Or soft blue-grays as thin as glancing waves.
(I've dreamt that water nymphs were dressed
    like that.)
Or take the color that resembles saffron,
Transparent as the dew Aurora wears,
The kind of dress she fancies when she mounts
Bridle and bit on her dawn-breaking horses,
Or soft pale greens like the Paphian myrtle,
Or violet like the brilliant amethyst,
Or white-rose-belted-in-cream, or dazzling white-
    ness
Seen in the flight of cranes from northern Thrace.
(Nor, Amaryllis, are your colors gone:
The almond tints, and brave bright chestnut
    browns,
Or natural shades in honey-colored wools.)
Then choose your colors as you'd pluck gay
    flowers,
As variable as those earth wears in Spring
(Slow Winter dwindles as pink buds appear).
From many colors as these to tint your dresses,
And many more, then take your choice, my dears,
To suit yourselves. Each girl should know her
    colors!

Smoke-gray is wonderful for white-skinned girls
(Briseis was captured in a dark gray cloak);
And dark-skinned girls look marvelous in white
(White was the costume Andromeda wore
So well the Gods grew envious of her beauty
And doomed the island that was once her home).

Each girl should know the pleasures of her body
And how to use them when she falls in love:
Your beauties guide your style: a pretty face
Always looks best if girls lie on their backs—
But if your back looks better, hide your face;
Then show your pretty buttocks to your lover.
When Milanion mounted Atalanta,
He raised her lovely legs upon his shoulders;
If you have legs like hers, then get your lover
To do the same for you. A little girl
Should mount her friend and ride him like a pony.
But when a girl's as tall as Hector's wife,
She never rides on top to make him please her.
A woman whose long flanks invite attention
Should turn half-kneeling on the open bed,
Bend back her head and then receive her lover.
But if her thighs look young and her breasts
      perfect,
She should instruct her lover to stand up,
To mount her as she lies across the sheets.
Nor is it wrong then to let down your hair
Showing the raptures of a Phylleian mother
Her head sunk back in flowing locks around her.
If childbirth shows deep lines above your thighs
Then turn about, and like swift Parthian horses,
Take the delight that quickens your behind.
I know a thousand ways of making love:
One that is easy, never makes you weary,
Is resting half-reclined on your right side—
Of course there're many more. But of these arts
Not even Phoebus' oracles at Delphi,
Nor Ammon with horns sprouting from his head

Could give you more than what my Muse fore-
 tells.
These arts my lifework; if my long career
At making love means anything at all,
I speak the truth—my poems proof of it.
A woman when she gives herself to love
Should feel the deepest raptures of her being,
Should be love's act herself and melt away
To join her lover's exquisite delight.
Then she should make sweet sounds and little
 noises
And name the places that her lover touches.
Even if Nature fails you with half measures
Of what your joy should be, deceive your lover;
Make all the little noises that enchant him—
(O poor unhappy girl if her sweet cunt—
That place where men and women find their
 haven—
Should not respond to love, pretend it does.)
Don't let him think you're lying: spread your legs;
Or moan and sigh and lure him with your eyes.
Look, naughty girl, that place is waiting, ready—
It speaks a secret language, all its own.
And if a woman gets her fill of glory
When she makes love and takes joy in her lover,
She's half-indifferent when she asks for money.
A few words more: as you make love, my dear,
Don't open every window in your room;
A woman's body is enhanced by shadows. •

ROM   THE CURES FOR LOVE

Love read the name of this, my latest book;
"More wars for me," said he, "more opposition—"
Then I replied, "Dear Cupid, don't blame me:
I'm your defender and devoted servant,
Your poet-laureate—I wear your colors
Not Diomedes who half-killed your mother
Till she was rescued by the God of War
And in his chariot made her flight to heaven.
While some young men grow cool, I'm filled with
    heat:
Ask me my avocation—I make love!

O I've taught lovers how to prove their skill,
And what was impulse once is now an art.
Dear boy, you know me well: I won't play traitor
To your great gifts or my own artfulness,
Nor shall new books undo my earlier work.
If there's a lover who delights in love,
He has my blessings—let him sail ahead,
Saved by a lucky wind.
                But if a man
Is captured, tortured, ruled by some mad woman,
I'll save his life—here's where my art comes in.
Why does a certain lover wear a rope
Around his neck and swing, a tearful object,
Hanging from high-pitched beams? Why does
    another
Tear at his breast and fall upon his sword?
Cupid, dear Lord of Peace, don't play with mur-
    der—
Unless some men are cured, they'll die of love—
Cure them at once and steer them free of death!

Sir Cupid, you're a boy—and boyish play
Shows Cupid at his best—not tragedy:
Your naked arrows look like shafts of war,
Yet they're untainted by the smell of blood.
Let your stepfather Mars do what he wills
To carve his victories with sword and spear—
Take up your mother's art; her artfulness
Would never kill another mother's son!

When you run out to play, unhinge that door
Which bars a midnight lover from his lady,
And dress his lady's gates with love-wreathed
    flowers:
Set up your arbors where a timid girl
No longer fears to meet her secret lovers;
Then make your famous cleverness outwit
The red-eyed wakefulness of many husbands.
And if a locked-out lover sings his sorrows,
His hopes, his blandishments, allow his tears
To save his life and wash your hands of guilt.
Love's torch should never light quick funeral
    pyres."
That was my speech. Love shook his glittering
    wings:
The golden boy smiled at me, "Write your
    book!"

Brood on disasters that your lady brought you,
Then count your losses with resentful eyes:
"She took my savings—not content with that,
She forced me to put up my house for sale.
And what a liar! I could never trust her;
How many times she locked her bedroom door
With me outside—while she received new lovers—
She spends her nights with thieves or jewelry
    salesmen,
Or someone who makes millions in cosmetics!"
Let her deflections simmer in your blood,
And where they cluster, seeds of hatred grow:
Think how she ruined you—if you're deep-bitten,
Your friends will find you eloquent enough!
Not long ago I met a charming girl
Who had no use for me. I took advice,
My own advice that's never known to fail,
The perfect medicine, the only cure,
And I, myself, a very sick physician.
Large doses helped: I dreamed of her for days,
Of what her flaws might be, of how she looked:

"What fearful legs she has," I said, "God save
        me!"—
Yet they were lovely—"O what awkward arms
The foolish creature flings around her head"—
Yet they were beautiful—"How squat she is"—
She happened to be slender—"How expensive!
That girl would wreck a Roman millionaire"—
This last thought worked; I almost came to hate
        her.
The difficulty is: flaws mix with beauties,
And by mistake we call her beauties flaws.
If you're inventive, make the worst you can
Of every feature that enchants your eyes:
If she's deep-breasted, call the woman fat:
If she's sun-tanned, make sure you call her black;
If thin and graceful—then she's skin-and-bones.

Say that she's shrewd, but don't admit she's clever;
And if she tells the truth, insist she's stupid.
And more than that: if the poor girl's ungifted
In any art, then flattery's your guide—
Make her perform; if she's tone-deaf and hoarse,
Beg her to sing—and if the girl lacks rhythm
Force her to dance till arms and legs grow weary.
Her speech is vulgar?—make her talk for hours!
She can't read music?—lead her to the lyre,
Give her the flute—and listen to disaster!
She stumbles when she walks?—then take her
        walking!
And if the girl has udders like a cow's,
Don't let her cover them, but praise their beauty.
Her teeth are bad?—joke with her, make her laugh,
And if her eyes grow red with little weeping,
Then make her blubber in a rain of tears.
It's sometimes good to find her unprepared:
On mornings when the heat of sun flares high,
Rush to her room—

                                (We're always charmed by
                                                dress:
All's hidden under veils, gold, precious stones,

The actual woman almost out of sight;
For gold, Love's aegis, dazzles every eye.)
Don't knock, walk in, yourself dressed to per-
    fection,
While the poor girl at toilet looks obscene
(And yet . . . and yet . . . take my advice with
    caution,
For naked artlessness tricks many lovers.)
See how she paints her face—don't fear to look—
Her eyelids, lips—all in a thousand colors,
Look where cosmetics trickle down her breasts.
The room reeks with her—hear me, Phineus!
Her dressing table smells as if the Harpies
Walked in to feed me half your poisoned dinner—
My stomach turns; the girl consults her mirror;
Nor this the first time that I'm feeling sick.

If my advice is not a waste of words,
If through my lips the genius of Apollo
Has anything to say, remember this:
Even though you burn like ancient Aetna's fires,
Address your lady like a sheet of ice;
You may feel half-insane, don't let her know it—
Laugh in her face and never show your tears.
(But if you're deep in love, forget advice;
My cures are never worse than your disease.)
Pretend you're not a lover—that your madness
Has almost flown away—you may be cured.
(To cure myself of drink, I've closed my eyes,
Put out the light and snored—and sure enough,
I sometimes fell asleep.)
                    See that poor fool:
He talked himself into a love affair
                              I've laughed
    aloud
To see a young man play the anguished lover
Only to fool himself: I saw him fall
In own trap, as helpless as a bird
Fed by his lady—there was no escape.

Love is a habit that some men acquire •
And possibly unlearn.
                        Deny love's madness
And you might be another man again.
Say she agrees to sleep with you tonight:
Tonight is here: you stand outside her door:
Her door is locked: don't try to break it down,
Nor plead, nor rail, nor spend the night outside,
But walk away.
                        Tomorrow morning's here:
Then meet her easily with cheerful words;
Your lack of eagerness'll make her humble—
That's your advantage—learned from Ovid's art!
But don't think that your love affair is over:
The horse half-broken-in may throw you yet.
Hide your advantage now: don't let her know it;
(A clever she-bird recognizes traps)
Let her be discontented with herself
And keep the upper hand. Sustain indifference.
On yet another night—
                        is her door open?
Though she calls out your name, walk straight
        away.
If she invites you, you have other dates.
Such trials are scarcely difficult at all—
Then when you leave her, take up other girls
Easy to get and glorious in bed! •

A bright young man who learned my cures for
        love,
Who practiced every rule my Muse advised him,
Who seemed in sight of port and free from harm,
Stepped out into a crowd of fervent lovers—
The boy was lost, back where his cures began,
Love's arrows pierced him everywhere he turned.
If you're in love and hope to be heart-free,
Don't meet with other lovers—they're con-
        tagious—
Even brute animals infect each other.

One look at those caught up in love's quick fever
Spreads the disease—our very eyes convey it—
And often we fall ill by accident.
Some rivers drop invisibly to shallows
By seeping into arid summer earth—
So waters run—so love creeps in unseen—

If you meet her again my work's undone!
O lovers are ingenious, sinuous creatures!

Another boy was cured: love's madness vanished:
And yet he haunted places where his lady
Walked out on afternoons—proximity
Unhinged his mind: the old wound opened up,
My arts were lost in one decisive battle.

If houses down the block are swept by fires,
Don't live next door, move to another street;
And if you stroll through marble colonnades,
Don't take the path your lady used to walk,
And never go to dinner with her friends—
Why force your memory, cooling in the shade,
To burst in flames of violent summer heat?
Give up this world—move to another planet!
If you've been half-starved for a week or two,
It's hard to break a date that offers dinner.
The very sight of fountains raises thirst!
And it's almost impossible to lead
A bull who sees a young and friendly cow;
The stallion whinnies at a well-groomed mare!
If cures are to be had, and you land safe,
A pilgrim on a convalescent shore,
It's not enough to leave the girl behind—
Don't see her mother, sister, maiden aunt,
Her childhood friends, her governess, her nurses,
(Who know her secrets) and pretend to weep.
Though you may long to ask them, don't inquire
If she is well or ill: be firm, be strong—
Better for you to be both deaf and dumb.
(Young men should never talk of how they fell

Or in or out of love, nor curse their women;
A courteous silence is the best revenge—
Slowly her image fades among your errors.)
Don't say your love has ended: close your lips,
For he who says too often, "Love is dead,"
Is still in love—better to let love's fires
Die down by slow degrees into pale ashes—
Then you are saved: a cloudburst has more force
Than drizzling rain, yet blinding showers are
    spent
Almost at once, while rain drifts down for hours.
Let love die by neglect in noiseless air.
Yet never hate the girl you loved too well—
That end of love is living like a beast:
Hate proves you're still in love—why spend your
    days
In hateful agonies? Walk free and easy
As though you were indifferent as the wind—
There's nothing more disgraceful than two lovers,
Man against woman, at continual war.

And here are miscellaneous cures for love:
Stray warnings, parables—and my advice:
In dangerous cases, some may be of help.
Imagine Phaedra poor and not a queen—
She'd have small chance at meeting Hippolytus—
Royal Neptune's grandson, nor would Neptune's
    bulls
Have caused the death of her escaping lover.
If Ariadne had not been a princess
Perhaps she would have made a wiser choice
Of lovers than her disappearing Theseus.
No one loved Hecate, no woman, Irus:
The reason why? Both creatures were too poor—
Irus, a beggar. Continual lack of money
Discourages a passionate love affair,
(This cure for love is scarcely worth your trouble
If you're compelled to walk about in rags.)
Avoid the theater—wait until your heart

Is drained of love—a shell of emptiness—
And stay away from zithers, flutes, and lyres,
The sound of voices making cheerful music,
And swaying dancing girls whose graceful arms
Keep time to sinuous rhythms. O the dance
Always enraptures the unwary lover—
That way is madness—and the actor's art
However much it holds you with delight
Warns you to leave at once—your place is home.
I hate to say it (for these words undo me)
Don't read the poets. Fly from Callimachus—
(For he's no enemy of love)—and Philetas—
If you read both together, you're destroyed.
And Sappho taught me how to please my women,
And the same Muse that warmed Anacreon
Turned me to fire and led me from discretion.
Who reads the songs of Tibullus unmoved?
Or Cynthia's poet, our Propertius?
Who can read Gallus and still walk iron-hearted?
Who can read me? . . . I am of their company,
Poet and lover in Apollo's line.

MENTOR Books of Special Interest

The Young Caesar *by Rex Warner*
In this brilliant novel by a noted classical scholar,
Caesar tells his own story of his youthful military
adventures and his rise to power. (#MT447—75¢)

The Roman Way to Western Civilization
by Edith Hamilton
A companion to *The Greek Way*, this book inter-
prets the heritage of Rome as revealed in the words
of her great writers. (#MP509—60¢)

Life Stories of Men Who Shaped History
from Plutarch's Lives, edited by E. C. Lindeman
A distinguished selection taken from the John and
William Langhorne translation. (#MP397—60¢)

The Aeneid *by Vergil, translated by Patric Dickinson*
The great Roman epic of adventure, war, and love,
in a brilliant new verse translation by a noted English poet and classical scholar. (#MT348—75¢)

The Greek Way to Western Civilization *by Edith
Hamilton.* A notable key to the achievements of ancient Greece in literature and art. (#MP513—60¢)

Mythology *by Edith Hamilton.* A brilliant re-telling
of the classic Greek, Roman, and Norse legends of
love and adventure. (#MP520—60¢)

War Commentaries of Caesar *translated by Rex
Warner.* Julius Caesar's classic first-hand account of
his military campaigns in an outstanding translation
by the author of *The Young Caesar.*
(#MT333—75¢)

The Civilization of Rome *by Donald R. Dudley.* A
cultural and social history of Rome from the earliest
time to the fall of the empire. (#MT472—75¢)